Carolyn –

Be great and always
trust your Own Chapter!

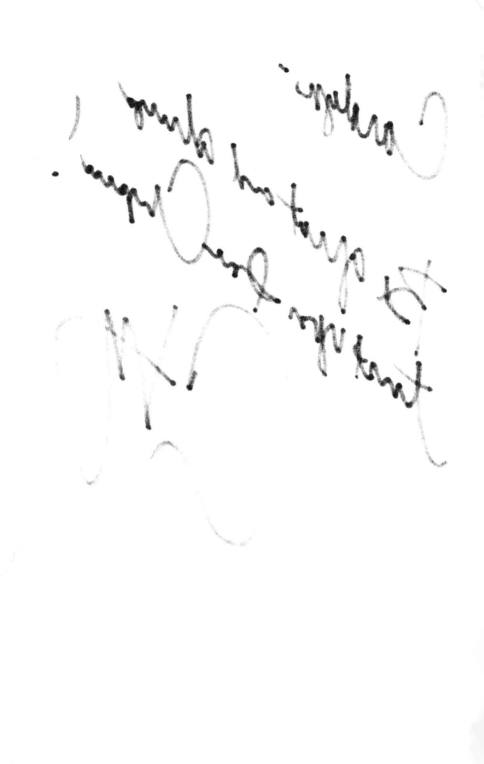

Black Belt Leadership

Chris Natzke

Black Belt Leadership:
7 Keys to Creating a Life of Purpose
by Discovering Your Inner Champion
By Chris Natzke

Published by Spiritco Press™
Aurora, CO

Natzke, Chris, Author
Black Belt Leadership:
7 Keys to Creating a Life of Purpose
by Discovering Your Inner Champion

Cover Design: NZ Graphics, Inc.
Interior Design: Andrea Costantine
Editor: Angela Renkoski

ISBN 978-1489552976

1. Leadership 2.Self-improvement 3. Martial Arts

Black Belt Leadership

7 Keys to Creating a Life
of Purpose by Discovering
Your Inner Champion

Chris Natzke

7th Degree Black Belt, Master Instructor

*Mastery in our careers (and in our lives!) requires that
we constantly produce results beyond and out of the ordinary.
Mastery is a product of consistently going beyond our limits.
For most people, it starts with technical excellence in a chosen
field and a commitment to that excellence. If you're willing to
commit yourself to excellence, to surround yourself with things
that represent this excellence, your life will change.*
—Stewart Emery

*Knowing others is intelligence; knowing yourself is true wisdom.
Mastering others is strength; mastering yourself is true power.*
—Anonymous

DEDICATION

To my sons, Joshua and Jason,
I love you so much. You are my life's greatest gifts.
I am so honored to be your father.

ACKNOWLEDGMENTS

WE HAVE A SAYING IN MARTIAL ARTS THAT "NO one gets to Black Belt by themselves." It takes a team of committed and compassionate individuals to help any student attain the rank of Black Belt. Much like the martial arts, this project would never have come into being without the loving support of the many incredible people I am blessed to call friends, teachers, coaches and partners.

To my mother, Marianne Jonides, for all of your love and support and for teaching me to always go for my dreams. To my stepfather, Dan Jonides, for your loving kindness, strength and wisdom.

To Beth Asbury, for your amazing generosity in the editing of this book. To Angela Renkoski, for your professional editing expertise and loving support. To Polly Letofsky for your guidance and inspiration in making this book a reality.

To Sally McGhee, for your love and friendship in opening me up to a whole new part of myself. To Stephen and Doug McGhee for your brotherhood and constant reminder of what it is to be a powerful and loving man. To my men's group (Steve Ruskaup, Rich Crum, Barry Lewis, Arjay Jones, Dr. Greg Mortimer and Andy Johnson) for always encouraging me to be my best—*Ho!* To Craig Zablocki for helping me on the path to finding my real voice, which comes from my heart. To Joe Sabah and Diana Hall for your incredible support in helping me on the road to becoming a professional speaker.

To Dr. Roger Teel and the staff of Mile Hi Church, thank you: My life has been transformed by your teachings and love. To Lisa and Alan Iguchi, my sister and brother from another mother, thank you for always being there for me—I love you. To my Hawaiian brother and sister, Peter Happi and Barbara Lusardi, for teaching me the loving spirit of A*loha* – *Mahalo*. To Marilyn Brookhart, for your loving guidance and support throughout the years. To my brother, Sherif Sakr, thank you for always reminding me to powerfully walk my path, despite my fears and doubts.

To Drs. Ron and Mary Hulnick, thank you for your loving leadership and for sharing your wisdom through the University of Santa Monica. To my USM sisters, Michelle Scott, Kathy McMillin and Laurie Robinson, thank you for your loving support in the creation and completion of this project. To the Insight Seminars Denver community, thank you for teaching me to open my heart. To my brothers, Joey Hubbard and Peter Felsman, thank you for your constant example of living an Awakened Heart.

And finally, a big thank you to my martial arts family. To Grandmaster Jae Kyu Lee, thank you for always believing in me, sir; I don't know where I would be without you—*Pil Sung!* To the owners, students and staff of the Colorado Alliance of Martial Arts for your love and support and inspiring me to live my dreams. To Master Theresa Byrne, for your friendship, guidance and constant support and encouragement. To my friends, Masters Tom Callos and Dave Kovar, for teaching me to think outside the box and not take myself so seriously and for showing me the true meaning of personal mastery. To Bill "Superfoot" Wallace, thank you, sir, for teaching me to be a champion.

CONTENTS

INTRODUCTION. 19
"I Will Make You a Champion!". 23
Seven Qualities of Black Belt Leadership. 27

CHAPTER 1: PURPOSEFUL VISION. 31
Three Keys to Creating a Purposeful Vision. . . . 41
What is the Purpose of my Life?. 46
Areas of Impact Exercise 49
Living Vision Exercise. 52

CHAPTER 2: BE THE CHANGE. 55
Being the Change. 64
Shifting to a "Be/Do/Have" Mindset. 69
Clarity and Awareness Exercise. 72
Creating What You Want Exercise. 74

CHAPTER 3: INTEGRITY 79

The Power of Keeping Agreements. 87

The "5 D's" of Keeping Agreements. 89

The First D – Detail It. 90

The Second D – Delete It. 92

The Third D – Defer It. 93

The Fourth D – Delegate It. 93

The Fifth D – Do It. 94

CHAPTER 4: CONSCIOUS PERSISTENCE 97

Conscious Persistence. 101

Discipline Leads to Freedom. 102

Freedom Leads to Expansion. 106

Traveling the Road to Black Belt. 108

Expanding Your Comfort Zones. 110

Four Stages of Expansion. 111

CHAPTER 5: COMPASSIONATE SERVICE 123

Seeking First to Understand. 127

The Need for Compassionate Service. 131

Giving and Receiving Are the Same Energy. 133

My School of Compassionate Service. 136

Opportunities to Serve. 138

CHAPTER 6: ACCEPTANCE AND SURRENDER . . . 143

What We Resist Persists 147

Is the Ticket Good or Bad? 149

Acceptance and Surrender of Ourselves 152

The Story of the Watermelon Boy 153

Strength Comes from Vulnerability 157

Forgiveness 159

The Story of the Two Monks 163

CHAPTER 7: INSPIRED ACTION 167

Move the Body 170

Bazooka Joe's Wisdom 174

Black Belt Cycle of Success 176

Taking Inspired Action Exercise 183

Do It Anyway 184

EPILOGUE 187

INTRODUCTION

MASTERY. THROUGHOUT THE AGES, PEOPLE CON-
sidered to have high levels of mastery in their lives, craft or
art have been revered by multitudes for their contributions to
our world. What made these individuals truly extraordinary
is the fact that their mastery extended far beyond having simple command, great skillfulness or knowledge of a subject
or activity.

Rather, by achieving a profound level of excellence in
their work, they were able to impact others so deeply that
they became a source of inspiration for millions who followed. Not only did future generations enjoy and appreciate
these masters' unique contributions in the way of art, music
and science, but the example also gave those who followed
permission to expand on their original masterpieces and express themselves in even greater ways.

Although many of us may never realize the artistic skill
of a Michelangelo or the creative imagination of an Einstein,

we all have the capacity to become a master in our own way and to express our own unique gifts in the world.

For the past four decades, my chosen field of mastery has been martial arts. During this time, I honed my skills in the art of Tae Kwon Do until my body was finely tuned and my mind was sharp and responsive. Although I was able to attain great athletic feats, what has come present for me is that, as I dedicated myself to mastery of my art, the experience of growth and expansion was not limited to the development of my expertise in kicking and punching. In fact, as I focused my energy into the mastery of my martial art, the habits developed, the discipline forged and the lessons learned permeated all areas of my life.

The beauty here is that when allowed to expand, this gift of mastery of an art or craft becomes such a part of the fabric of our lives that it works as a platform to achieve something even greater—the true expression of Self. I have purposely capitalized the "S" in Self to make an important distinction. The small "s" self is the part of us that supports our ego and is swayed and impacted by the outside world. It is the self that produces the negative voices of worry and concern in our head, keeps us paralyzed in fear of moving in the direction of our dreams and places the value of others' opinions of us and our talents over our own inner knowing.

The big "S" Self, on the other hand, is the true expression of our being. It is our connection to Spirit that guides us on our divine mission on this planet. It is heard in the "still, small voice" of our intuition and is found in the loving knowingness that we are always safe. It is the part of us that resides in our heart and urges us to fully Self-express and share our gifts with the world. It is the part of us that truly knows we are extensions of God and we have never left our source.

As such, this Self-mastery is not confined to a particular craft or skill but becomes the application of Self-knowledge and expansion into higher levels of personal growth and consciousness. This Self-mastery brings forward the opportunity to exercise right action and make desired personal changes based on our choosing. Self-mastery is not only represented by what we do or what we possess, but it is also demonstrated as a powerful state of *being* in our daily living.

What's more, it is my belief that as we begin to attain higher levels of mastery in any endeavor, we also begin to realize there is still so much more to learn and experience. The truest of masters realize they are never finished learning and expanding but are always humble students. "The more I learn, the more I realize what I do not know" becomes our mantra. The road to mastery, therefore, never ends. When it is embraced and followed with humility and a sense of wonder, it expands our minds, opens our hearts and empowers our bodies to heights never before reached or imagined.

In the past seven decades in the United States, martial arts have grown from an activity brought over by G.I.s from post-World War II Asia and reserved for adults only to (thanks in large part to the *Karate Kid* movies) a discipline now associated with children that focuses on building focus, confidence and respect. In fact, martial arts are more popular than ever in history. With more than 70 million practitioners worldwide, martial arts are seen daily in movies, television shows, magazines and video games. The Black Belt, with more than 4 million practitioners across the globe holding this prestigious rank, has become a well-known symbol for discipline, perseverance, and, yes, mastery. No longer the obscure activity they were 40 to 50 years ago, martial arts are a familiar and recognizable piece of the fabric of our society.

When viewed from a limited context, martial arts may be seen only as a physical activity, a method of self-protection or a means of settling conflict through physical force. However, in the past four decades, I have found martial arts to be so much more. They have served as a path to deep, profoundly personal introspection and expansion. In fact, martial arts have provided not only the platform for my personal development and growth but also the means by which I share my unique gifts with the world.

As you picked up this book, you might have been wondering, how can martial arts principles help me in my quest for personal mastery? Doesn't one have to train for decades to realize the true benefits of the martial arts? Can I truly understand and assimilate the principles into my life simply by reading a book?

These are valid questions. However, it is not my intention in writing this book to make you an expert martial arts practitioner or even a proficient student. It is my intention to share with you the life principles and practices I have found to be the key components of my personal happiness, expansion and success. Regardless of whether one has ever learned to throw a kick or a punch, martial arts principles, when practiced and assimilated, are not about achieving purely physical mastery; they are about accessing your *Inner Champion*.

The Merriam-Webster dictionary defines a *champion* as someone who is a "warrior or fighter, winner of first place or first prize in a competition." Although this is an accurate description of a competitive athlete succeeding in life's outer realm, what I am talking about is a journey we master as a champion inside ourselves that eventually leads us to producing results in the outer world. It is my belief that it is from our *Inner Champion* that our personal qualities of greatness have their genesis. It is and always has been available to us. It is simply a matter of conscious choice, inner nurturing and discipline that allow our *Inner Champion* to emerge. This is my story of its emergence and impact on my life.

"I WILL MAKE YOU A CHAMPION"

I participated in my first class in the martial art of Tae Kwon Do on September 13, 1973, at the age of 10. I remember this date clearly, as it was my brother Danny's fifth birthday, and I had received special permission from my mother to miss his birthday party to take my first lesson in Korean Karate.

Like many boys my age, I had been inspired by the television show *Kung Fu*. In it, actor David Carradine, playing Shaolin monk Kwai Chang Caine, roamed the desert of the Western United States. In each town he entered, bad-guy cowboys took exception to Caine's presence and chose to inflict their force upon him. Each episode included a physical showdown where Caine, reluctant to use his martial arts skills, would handle his unruly adversaries with expert punches, kicks and throws. Having killed the Chinese emperor's son for viciously slaying his beloved teacher, the blind Master Po, Caine found it necessary to be a man on the run to stay alive. As a result, each episode ended with Caine fleeing to the next town, looking to stay one step ahead of the bounty hunters who pursued him.

Each episode also included teachings of martial arts philosophies delivered through flashbacks in the Shaolin monastery of "Grasshopper," the nickname Caine had received as a young student, listening to the wise counsel of his two teachers, Masters Kan and Po. A typical scene shared wisdom this way:

Young Caine: You cannot see.

Master Po: You think I cannot see?

Young Caine: Of all things, to live in darkness must be worst.

Master Po: Fear is the only darkness.

After all these years of life experience, just reading that last quote gives me chills. I now realize that those wisdom-filled flashbacks were probably the richest value of the show. However, as a starstruck 10-year-old, they did not interest me all that much. It was the fighting I loved. I dreamed of one day being able to possess those masterful martial arts skills of the Shaolin monk Kwai Chang Caine.

After weeks of begging and pleading with my mother, I finally was allowed to attend my first martial arts class. I remember it as if it were yesterday. The strong and powerful movements, precise kicking and striking, and visceral *ki haps* (spirit yells) rang through the air. As I sat cross-legged on the floor observing the senior students, a feeling of exhilaration coursed through my body. I truly felt I had come home.

About three years after this first class, I met a man who changed my life forever. His name was Grandmaster Jae Kyu Lee. Master Lee had recently come from Korea. He had little money in his pocket and a limited use of the English language, but he possessed a burning desire to transform lives through the martial arts.

Before one of the first classes I attended with Master Lee, I was seated on the floor in the back of the room. My legs were spread wide as I stretched and loosened up my muscles for the vigorous training ahead. As he walked by, Master Lee stopped and looked curiously at me. Soon he was seated on the floor in front of me. He then proceeded to put his right foot on the inside of my left leg, his left foot on the inside of my right leg. Quickly grabbing the ends of my belt, in one fluid push-pull movement, he split me out to 180 degrees!

I learned two things that day. The first is that anyone can do the splits—once. The second and most important lesson came when Master Lee looked me deeply in the eyes and said to me in his broken English, "*I will make you a champion.*" I will make you a champion. I fell still as his words penetrated my being. I was deeply moved. As a 13-year-old, all I could think about at the time were medals, trophies and Olympic glory. I remember floating home that day to tell my parents what Master Lee had promised me. I was to become a champion!

It has been more than three-and-a-half decades since Master Lee said those life-changing words. I eventually would experience much success in the martial arts arena, culminating with a national championship in 1999, but I have come to realize Master Lee's words had much deeper meaning and his message was much more profound, far beyond arenas and trophies. What he was communicating to me was a principle he frequently referred to as becoming a "Life Champion," someone who could set powerful goals and achieve them, someone who could move through life's adversity with strength and grace, and most important, someone who could live a life of service to others. When Master Lee said, "I will make you a champion," I actually heard and felt to the core of my being, "I believe in you." Thus, was my *Inner Champion* awakened.

It is from this teaching that my personal philosophy of happiness and success was born. I have summed these up in the following principles I call the Seven Qualities of Black Belt Leadership. These have been the guiding values of my life and are integral to the teachings of the martial arts school I founded. I have been honored to teach thousands of students these principles and have watched in awe as wonderful changes flow into their lives. It is my honor to share them with you.

SEVEN QUALITIES OF BLACK BELT LEADERSHIP

1. Purposeful Vision: *Gaining clarity of and committing to a life vision that has purpose and meaning for you*

2. Be the Change: *Powerfully moving through life as an expression of who you want to "be" in the world*

3. Personal Integrity: *Realizing the impact of honoring your word not only to others but, more important, to your Self*

4. Conscious Persistence: *Realizing freedom comes through discipline while expanding gracefully out of your comfort zone and into transformation*

5. Compassionate Service: *Making a difference in the world through empowered empathy*

6. Acceptance and Surrender: *Letting go of your fears, judgments and what no longer serves you to embrace a life perspective that leads to peace, clarity and transformation*

7. Inspired Action: *Activating strength of heart and taking the steps necessary to realize your dreams and impact the world*

These qualities have been with me at the very best times of my life—in becoming a 7th Degree Black Belt, winning a national championship and creating a very successful martial arts business. More important, they were there for me when life wasn't so good—at age seventeen, when I lost my younger brother Danny to a drowning accident; later when I went through a very painful divorce after a 26-year relationship and earlier when I grew up in a household where my father couldn't overcome the disease of alcoholism that haunted him his entire life. During these difficult times, I truly needed to live from the Seven Qualities of Black Belt Leadership and access my *Inner Champion*.

I am grateful for the experiences that led to my accessing and expanding my *Inner Champion*, the limitless power that lives within each and every one of us and awaits our discovery. As I said, one doesn't need to know how to throw a punch or execute a powerful kick to access the *Inner Champion*—what one does need to be aware of is that this part of the Self exists. We were put on this planet to be the fullest expression of who we were meant to be. Regardless of the circumstances a person grew up in, one's socioeconomic background or whatever place one finds him or herself in today, the *Inner Champion* lives inside the heart and is waiting to express. The greater the emergence of our *Inner Champion*, the greater the positive impact we will experience here in our physical world.

We have a saying in martial arts that a "champion doesn't need to be told what to do; he/she only needs to be reminded." Remember that saying as you are reading this book and immersing yourself in the Qualities of Black Belt Leadership. Keep it in mind as you embark on the exercises in the book or as you are reflecting on how you can embrace each of these qualities in your own life. Let it act as a reminder that all of the answers to life's challenges already are present inside of you.

Your own *Inner Champion* is ready to come forward. It may come in a whisper or it may come in one grand moment. It may be something you have known your whole life or something that comes to you in a state of profound inspiration. Regardless of how your *Inner Champion* makes itself known to you, please remember the only thing limiting you is the level of trust, belief and compassion you hold for yourself. The only thing preventing you from experiencing your own unique form and expression of mastery unfolding is ***you***. Let's begin now to unlock your personal mastery by discovering the *Inner Champion* inside of you.

1

PURPOSEFUL VISION

If one advances confidently in the direction of his dreams,
and endeavors to live the life which he has imagined,
he will meet with success unexpected
in common hours.
—Henry David Thoreau

IT IS OFTEN SAID THAT WITHOUT A VISION, THE people will perish. Each day when we wake up, we have a choice as to the life we want to create. We are beings, powerful beyond measure, but what we forget to realize is so much (if not all) of what we experience in life is of our own creation.

When things are going well in our lives, it is easy to take credit for the creations. When business is good, it is because of our own foresight and hard work. When relationships are going well, it is because of our full intention in creating love, harmony and joy between ourselves and another person. When our health is vibrant and sound, it is because we have chosen to exercise and eat right.

But what about those times in our life when things aren't going so well? What about when your business is struggling to meet its expenses, much less grow? It must be the economy, poor marketing or the lack of skill and effort of my employees, we tell ourselves. What about when relationships become filled with conflict? It has to be the other person who has the issues; it can't be me. And when health begins to falter? It must be the environment, the diet my wife feeds me or just old age.

Even those life experiences that seem tragic and out of our control actually have an origin in how we think, intend and believe our lives to be. Even if we believe we have absolutely no control of the circumstances we find ourselves in, we absolutely do have great power in how we choose to respond to them. Please consider, for a moment, that every experience in our lives we actually create, promote or allow.

In giving direct attention, action or thought, we are always actively in the mode of *creation* in our lives. When we put ourselves in situations that *promote* the probability of something happening just by being present (e.g. being in a bad area of town) or we *allow* things to continue to happen in our lives because we refuse to take a stand for ourselves (e.g. a bad or abusive relationship), we do bear responsibility for what occurs.

So many of us have created a vision for ourselves based primarily on what others have told us is "true." We tend to limit ourselves and our lives, giving far too much credence to what others have said is possible. We are influenced by our parents, teachers and coaches. Friends and siblings often have a tremendous impact on our beliefs, tainting how we see ourselves. Even the news media and collective consciousness of our times have a tremendous impact on our vision.

I have come to believe that what I focus on in my life expands, and nothing can have a greater impact on that than a **purposeful vision**. I use the term purposeful to denote an intent or deliberate choice to create what we want in our lives. What I am talking about is deliberately choosing to create from that which is inside you, from your Self, to skillfully and appropriately ignore all those outside influences that limit you. When we choose a vision for our lives that inspires us, motivates us, excites us and supports us in our expansion and growth, we tend to get more of those experiences in our lives that support this vision. By the same token, when we focus on the hardships, difficulties and struggles in our lives, or the "negative" influences of the day, we tend to get more of these types of things showing up in our experiences.

Play a little game with me. Take a moment and look around the room and notice everything that is the color *blue*: possibly a blue shirt, a blue wall, blue sky, blue in a painting or upholstery. Thoroughly try to identify everything you see that is even the slightest shade of blue.

Great, now close your eyes for thirty seconds and begin to remember everything you saw that was the color *pink*. Yes, I said "pink." Go ahead, close your eyes and give it a try. OK, it is challenging to do, isn't it? How many things could you list that were pink? One, two, maybe none? You see, when I asked you to focus on the color blue, you weren't focusing on the color pink. You had shut down your capacity to notice items of that color. In essence, it was a choice in how you were focusing your attention that was the real key. Likewise, a choice of focus is key when you are creating your purposeful vision for your life.

For example, have you ever wanted a new car? Can you picture it now, the make, the model, the color? Recently, I made the decision that I wanted a hybrid Lexus SUV. Gold was my preferred color. As soon as I made that choice, what did I begin to see on the road? Of course, I saw Lexus SUVs everywhere.

This concept came into my awareness many years ago when I first got the news I was going to be a father. Picture this: I was 21 years old, a newlywed and student-athlete at Northwestern University in Evanston, Illinois. As a linebacker for the football team, I was dutifully focusing on my studies and preparing for the upcoming Saturday game against Ohio State University. My new wife suddenly bounced through the door with a smile and announced, "I'm pregnant. We are going to have a baby!"

I responded like any young man just learning he was going to be a father by exclaiming, "Yes! I am going to be a dad!" This was immediately followed by my worrisome thoughts of "Oh, my God, I am going to be a dad." With these thoughts in my consciousness, you can probably guess what I saw when I went out later in the day. That's right— PREGNANT WOMEN! They were everywhere. They were walking down the street, they were in the grocery stores, and they were at the gym. It was as if a spaceship had landed and deposited a massive group of expectant mothers to take over our planet. But they were actually always there before, weren't they? They just had not been in my consciousness and, therefore, not in my present awareness.

Following this principle means you do need to be careful what you focus on and what you want to ask to create in your world. I grew up in a small town in the Midwest called Oconomowoc, Wisconsin. It has the distinct honor of being the only city in the United States with five O's in its name: O-C-O-N-O-M-O-W-O-C. (There will be a quiz on its spelling at the end of this chapter.) This little community, located 30 miles west of Milwaukee, is a beautiful place, nestled among three lakes with a genuine feel of small town Americana.

A couple lived there named Dr. John and Mary Smith,

who were beloved in the community. Dr. Smith was a local pediatrician and had delivered what seemed to be an entire generation of children. Mary, along with managing the doctor's office, was deeply involved in the community. She could often be seen organizing the efforts of the town fair or leading the Junior League charity fund-raisers.

One July, a special event was about to take place. Dr. and Mrs. Smith had been born just a couple of days apart and were about to celebrate their 60th birthdays. They were also set to celebrate their 40th wedding anniversary. The entire town was preparing to come to the local park to celebrate with the Smiths. Casseroles, cakes and bratwursts were all being diligently prepared to support the big event at the park.

That morning, the Smiths were in their bedroom getting dressed for the gala. Dr. Smith was prepping in front of a full-length mirror, hair neatly slicked back, wearing his signature bow tie and his best summer suit. Mary was adorned in a beautiful sundress, wonderfully accompanied by a gorgeous hat and her radiant smile. As she put the final touches on her lipstick, something amazing happened—a fairy appeared to them. That's right, a fairy (just stay with me). Although surprised and a little frightened, the Smiths were soon smoothed by the fairy's angelic voice as she said to them:

"John and Mary Smith, you are so beloved in this community. You have given so much of yourself in a loving and unselfish way and you are about to be rewarded. I would like to offer you each a wish, for whatever you want, a thank you for your unwavering kindness and service."

Well, although still a little off balance from the surprise of such a visitor, Mary quickly collected herself and said emphatically, "I know what I want. I want two round-trip tickets around the world!" She had grown up in this little two-horse town and had a deep yearning to shake its dirt from her feet and see the world.

The fairy said, "Very well," waved her magic wand and instantly, two round-trip tickets around the world appeared in Mary's delicate hands.

Dr. Smith was a little taken aback with all of this. He looked at his wife then he looked at his feet; he looked at the fairy then he looked back at his feet. Finally, his head rose up with a snap and he turned to the fairy and proclaimed, "I know what I want. I want a woman who is 30 years younger!"

A look of shock and dismay spread over Mary's face. The fairy, however, calmly nodded her head and said, "Very well." She waved her magic wand and instantly, John was 90 years old.

OK, so maybe this story did not actually take place, but it clearly illustrates the care we need to take in setting our intentions. We are powerful creators. In fact, we are always creating. Both the "positive" and the "negative" experiences we have in our lives come as a result of our conscious intentions, subconscious thoughts or the judgments we place on what we are experiencing. It is our responsibility to monitor our thoughts, beliefs and actions. In doing this, we will create what we want to manifest in our lives.

When I first opened my professional martial arts school in

1995, the Family Martial Arts Center, it was both an exciting and terrifying time. Having never owned my own business and having left the comforts of the corporate haven, I had huge doubts and fears about being able to succeed. The added pressure of a wife and two young sons to support was at times overwhelming. Eventually, I got over myself and opened up the business, but in its early stages, I had my doubts and fears surface and, occasionally, overtake me.

One day that changed. I was standing in the office of the school and peering out onto the mats where three kids were stretching out before class. Suddenly, I found myself over-come with anxiety about making the business work. I was then struck by irony: There I was standing in my office with my knees shaking, wondering if I had what it took to be suc-cessful, and I was the one these parents had entrusted to teach their children confidence, goal setting and moving through life's obstacles.

In that moment I made the commitment that crystallized my vision for my new business and, I believe, changed my life. I promised myself that regardless of the actual number of students I had participating in a class, I would teach with the same energy and enthusiasm I would have if twenty students were on the mat. From that day forward, even if I experienced a difficult day or had only one student in my class, I was dedi-cated to giving my absolute best. I would hold my vision of creating the martial arts school of my dreams in all that I did.

I am happy to report that after only one year, I had more than 200 students attending my facility. To put that in perspective, the average martial arts school in 1995 served only eighty students. Within the next five years, the school had grown to more than 500 students and was one of the largest martial arts schools in Colorado. What made our school grow at a such an outstanding level compared to other new businesses? Well, it certainly wasn't the marketing. I sometimes have to chuckle when I look back at my poor attempts at advertising. It wasn't the location either. We were not situated in the heart of the city but on a moderately busy intersection surrounded by neighborhoods. I am convinced that it was about who I was being, how I had made the conscious choice to show up every day with complete devotion to my purposeful vision. I adhered to this vision. It was crystallized in my heart and mind, and my commitment to bringing it to life was *the* true difference in realizing my dream.

So what makes a purposeful vision come into reality? Certainly, taking inspired action to make things happen is important and will be explored in a later chapter. However, I believe that things in our lives are actually created twice. First, they are created in our consciousness then in our physical world reality. It is when these two elements are combined—a purposeful vision (consciousness) with inspired action (reality)—that magic can happen in our world. As noted futurist and author Joel Barker stated:

Vision without action is a dream. Action without vision is simply passing the time. Action with Vision is making a positive difference.

It has been my experience that a purposeful vision is fueled and supported by the following three factors.

THE THREE KEYS TO
CREATING A PURPOSEFUL VISION

1. It comes from your heart. The most powerful visions are those that come from deep within us, an urge or a yearning that needs to be expressed. They are not something we feel compelled to do based on social norms, a quick way to make money or another's expectation of us. A purposeful vision is something that comes from our heart; it touches us on a deeply emotional level. These purposeful visions are what we feel compelled to create as expressions of our true "Self." Many times these visions bring up a massive latent fear as we think of all of the reasons they might fail, and we doubt our capacity to fulfill our dreams. Purposeful visions take courage to dream. They take courage to create. It has often been said that courage is not the lack of fear, but taking action while having the fear. Those who have taken even a first year of high school French classes know the root of the word courage, is *coeur*, which means "heart." What is your heart telling you to create? What is the heartfelt vision for your life?

2. It is clearly defined in your mind. If our hearts are the source of our visions, our minds are the sculptors that help make them a reality. Visualization in our minds is a powerful tool for creating what we want to make manifest. Years ago, a University of Chicago study was done to measure the power of visualization. Several college students were brought to a gymnasium and were asked to begin shooting free throws from 15 feet away from the basketball hoop. A record was kept of the number of baskets made by each participant within a time period. Once all the results were noted, the students were broken into three groups for the rest of the study. One group was to practice shooting free throws 30 minutes each day, Monday through Friday, for four weeks. Another group was instructed to refrain from even picking up a basketball, much less, practice any free throws, for the next month. The final group was asked to simply visualize taking and successfully making free throws for 30 minutes each day for the four week duration of the experiment.

At the end of the trial period, each group returned to the gym and attempted to complete as many successful free throws as possible. As expected, the group which physically practiced free throws each day had the greatest level of improvement (24%) while those who had done nothing had no increase in performance. However, to the amazement of the experiment facilitators, the group which had simply visualized making free throws each day showed a 23% level of improvement, almost the exact level of those who had practiced physically during the study.

I do not take this experiment to mean that we never have to take physical initiative to realize our dreams. I do think, however, that it speaks to the power of our imaginations in creating what we want to achieve. As a competitive athlete, martial arts instructor/student, speaker and life coach, I have used the power of visualization numerous times over the years. The visualization preparation that I have done prior to my athletic events, conversations and speeches has undoubtedly resulted in greater success.

What is your vision for a certain aspect of your life? What does it look like, feel like, taste like? How would it positively impact you and those around you? Getting a clearly defined vision is a powerful tool, one we will explore with an exercise at the end of this chapter.

3. *You become it on the inside before it happens on the outside.* Realizing our visions is not just about taking logical actions or simply following detailed instructions. It is not about remaining stationary and simply dreaming about what we want. It is actually about *being* who we want to become even before we can actually see the evidence of change in our environment. When the number of martial arts students rocketed to 200 at my school within the first year, I was convinced that the most important component of that success was my commitment to playing the role of a successful martial arts school owner. I was living in and being that vision even before it was actualized. Some might call it "faking it until you make it"; some might call it "active visualization." I call it "*being* the change" you wish to see in your world.

Quite some time ago, I heard this story about actor Jim Carrey that beautifully illustrates this point. A native Canadian, Carrey had moved to Los Angeles to make it in the entertainment industry, setting his sights on being a major movie star. Carrey enjoyed a close relationship with his father, Percy. Even when the pressures of Tinsel Town discouraged him, his father gave him unwavering support. Carrey's father kept reminding him how much he believed in him, always letting his son know that he knew he would be a star one day.

Carrey experienced moderate success starring in the television shows *In Living Color* and *The Duck Factory* and acting in his first movie, *Once Bitten*. Carrey's first starring role in a big film, *Ace Ventura, Pet Detective*, followed. His career seemed to be on a roll, but just as fast as it took off, it came crashing down. He soon found himself running out of money and questioning whether his career would ever take off and sustain itself. All the while, his father's voice continued to play in his mind saying, "I believe in you."

One night, Carrey found himself in despair, short on cash with bills to pay and with no new job opportunities on the horizon; he was ready to call it quits and go back home to Canada. He got into his car and continued to drive into the night. Eventually he found himself on the top of Mulholland Drive at the site of the Griffith Observatory. There, while looking over Hollywood, he knew he was at a crossroads. Was he to stay in LA and continue the pursuit of his dream? Or was he to let it go and return home? Just when he was about to call it quits, he once again recalled his father's loving words of encouragement and something inside him stirred. He visualized himself experiencing massive success as a Hollywood star, and he recommitted himself on the spot to giving his movie career one last try.

Carrey replayed in his mind his father's words, almost like a mantra. These words flowed into his heart until he owned the greatness that was inside of him. He was committed to *being* the successful star he knew himself to be. As a way of affirming this belief, he took out a note card and replicated a check that was to be paid to the order of Jim Carrey; he post-dated it for Thanksgiving Day 1995. It was in the amount of $10 million. He placed it in his wallet and made his way back home, all the while hearing his father's voice: "I believe in you."

The weeks passed until one day a representative from Warner Brothers contacted Carrey's agent about his possible interest in starring in a new film called *The Mask*. The news delighted his father to no end. Carrey's zany antics were again in demand. Once released, in July of 1994, *The Mask* would become Carrey's biggest hit to date. Interestingly enough, the amount he was offered for this starring role was the exact amount he had written in the check to himself only a few months before—$10 million. Only three days after being contacted by Warner Brothers, Carrey's father suddenly became ill and died. Standing over his father's casket to say his last goodbye, Carrey reached into his jacket and pulled out his wallet. He took his handwritten $10 million "check" and placed it in his father's suit breast pocket. Carrey knew his father had given him the greatest gift one could ever receive: the gift of believing in his inner vision, in his dream, in his Self.

WHAT IS THE PURPOSE OF MY LIFE?

For some, creating a purposeful vision for one's life is an effortless task. They are extremely clear on the purpose of their life and why they were put on this earth. They know the gifts and skills they have to contribute and how they want to share them with the world. From this point, the creation of purposeful vision can be somewhat easy, flowing from the depths of one's heart and coming clear in one's imagination.

However, what happens when one's life purpose is not so clear? What happens when the questions of, Why am I here? What gifts am I supposed to share? And what really makes my heart sing? continue to banter about in our minds. In one's quest for creating a purposeful life vision, receiving the answers to these important questions becomes a prerequisite in creating a scene that supports one's path to personal Self-expression.

With this being the case, one could say that the first step in creating a purposeful vision in our lives is to clearly understand our *life's purpose*. We can start with the age-old question "What is the meaning of my life?"

Many journeys have been traveled in the quest to find oneself and understand the meaning of life. This "meaning of life" is different for each of us, as we are unique expressions of the Divine. Although there is nothing wrong with going on excursions to other parts of the world in hopes of discovering this, what lies within and the answers we seek are almost always found to be already within ourselves. Or as poet T. S. Eliot so eloquently wrote in *The Four Quarters*:

We shall not cease from exploration
And the end of all our exploring
Will be to arrive where we started
And know the place for the first time.

The same holds true for discovering our own life purpose. My experience has been that my life purpose was not something I needed to go out and find. Rather, it was something that I had been living my entire life.

"How can this be?" you might ask yourself, especially when you are feeling lost and unsure what path in life to take, much less a life vision you want to create. The truth is, none of us lives in a "purposeless" way. Up until this point in our lives, each of us has expressed our true life purpose at times—we just might not be aware of it. To illustrate this, I invite you to take some quiet time and deeply ask your *Inner Champion* the following questions. Listen openly to the answers.

- When were you doing or contributing something in your life that made you feel totally …
    happy?
    excited?
    energized?
    fulfilled?
- What were you doing?
- Who were you with?
- How were you contributing to others?
- What was the underlying purpose for these activities?

Once you have taken the time to answer these questions thoroughly, take a look at the common thread that exists in these instances. For example, were you teaching others? Were you guiding others how to move through difficult times? Were you expressing your joy through music? Were you expressing physically through dance or exercise? Were you solving complex problems?

When this exercise is done, people usually find that although the instances might differ in content, there is a common thread. The basic theme of all that brought you satisfaction and joy will remain constant. In doing this exercise for myself, I realized that during my life, I felt most alive and felt the most joy when I was *teaching, leading or inspiring* others to achieve happiness. This showed up in many ways. It was present in my work, in my relationships, in my athletic endeavors and in my martial arts practice and instruction. It had existed from the time I was a young boy into my teenage years and adulthood. The net realization was clear. My life purpose was not something I found because of a single job, career or activity I had embarked upon. Rather, it was the underlying theme of my life. I, just like you, have been *living* my purpose my whole life, even if I was not entirely aware that was what I was doing.

From this point of awareness, you can now ask yourself, "What is the purpose of my life?"

Areas of Impact Exercise

From the point of understanding your unique life purpose, you are now ready to begin creating Purposeful Visions for the various areas of your life. To begin, it is important to know where you are right now. Knowing where you started from will give you a clearer idea of where you would like to go. Using Figure 1 below, identify your starting point, or your current life experience, in the following eight key Areas of Impact: Relationships (family, spouse, significant others), Career Satisfaction, Service (charities, church, service organizations), Spiritual Connection, Health/Wellness, Material Things (home, car, toys), Leisure (vacations, recovery time) and Financial Well-being. Although this does not list all areas of life, it covers the major areas people focus on when reviewing the levels of effectiveness and happiness their lives.

Figure 1

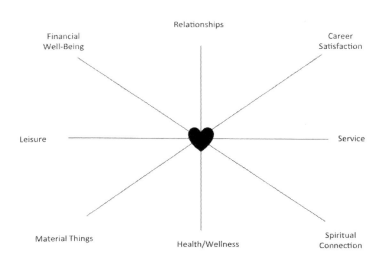

Next, plot a point on the chart that rates each life area on a scale of zero to 10, with zero being "highly dissatisfied" and 10 being "highly satisfied." With the heart center of the graph being zero, plot each life area. For example, in Figure 2, Financial is at a level "5," Relationships is at a level "9" and Leisure is at a level "3."

Figure 2

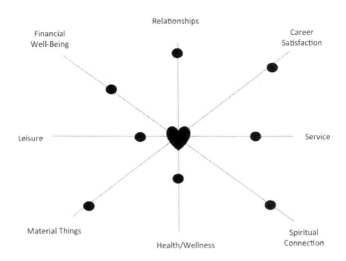

In the final step, shown in Figure 3, connect the plot points to get a visual of where you believe your life to be at the present moment. In a perfect world, where all aspects of your life are at a level 10, the figure would represent a perfect circle reaching out to the outer edges of the graph. However, in this example, it is clear there are areas that seem to be working relatively well (e.g. Relationships, Career, Material Things and Spiritual Connection). However, this person identified areas of opportunity in having what they want in their lives in the areas of Finances, Service, Leisure and Health/Wellness.

Figure 3

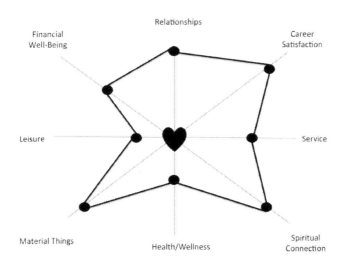

This graph could change from month to month, week to week and even day to day based on what is occurring in your life, how you feel and the judgments you make about current circumstances. Whatever you identify, simply start where you are and move forward from that point. Often, we don't take the time to see where we are and create a vision and plan for where we want to be. This process allows you to take a closer look at what you are currently creating in your world, which sets the stage for where you go next.

Living Vision Exercise

Now that you have a clear picture of where your life is, it is time to create your Purposeful Vision. In doing so, you will be able to move forward in the eight key areas.

Go to a quiet place, one in which you will not be disturbed. Turn off your phone and free yourself from any other distractions that might interrupt you. Allow yourself to relax into this special time, time you are giving to yourself. Light a candle. Sit at a table with paper and pen ready. Sitting up straight in your chair, with feet flat on the floor and eyes closed, begin to connect with your breath. As you inhale deeply from your nose, feel your breath reach all the way down to your belly. As you exhale through your mouth, feel all tension leave your body. When you begin to feel yourself relax, say a short prayer asking for guidance on this journey of self-discovery. Set an intention for receiving the perfect guidance in understanding your Purposeful Vision, for receiving a crystal clear understanding of what your Self wants to create in this lifetime of yours.

Once you feel relaxed and centered, choose one of the eight key areas previously explored, Career Satisfaction, for example. While placing your hand on your chest and focusing on your heart area, ask yourself the question, "If I were truly happy and fulfilled in my career, what would it look like?" Then—here comes the most important part—JUST LISTEN and allow the images to come into your mind. If any negative thoughts arise, thoughts of how difficult it might be or how many sacrifices you will have to make or what it might cost, thank the thoughts for sharing and allow them to pass on.

Gently bring your mind back to the visions of fulfillment. See the pictures clearly in your mind and begin to feel what it would be like to have exactly what your heart desires. What would your body feel like? How joyful would you feel? How amazing would it be to share yourself in the world in this way? Completely bask in the feeling of already having this vision manifested in the world.

When you feel this process is complete, gently open your eyes. Pick up your pen and begin writing exactly what vision came forth in your mind. Be intent on writing exactly what came forward for you, being careful to not allow any limiting thoughts about how this might be completed or how this vision might not be possible. Fully allow yourself to dream as if there were no limitations. If you knew you could not fail in this endeavor and you got everything you wanted, what would you have?

Once you feel the first life area Purposeful Vision is completed, gently place the pen down, close your eyes and repeat this process for the next life area, for example, Relationships. Allow the vision to unfold in your mind and listen to your heart to guide you in creating the vision.

After you have completed this process for each of the eight areas, take some time to review what you have written. Allow it to sink into your being. Bring yourself to a state in which you are feeling as if you had all of these wonderful things present in your world. Immerse yourself in the feelings of complete fulfillment. Wallow in the thoughts of how many people you are serving as you live in this perfect alignment with your true Self. Feel the pure joy and excitement of being YOU!

Now that you have documented your Purposeful Vision, it is important that this remains a working document you review and integrate regularly. You might feel more comfortable in typing up your Purposeful Vision and putting them in a prominent place that can be accessed easily. For those who are more visual, creating a vision board that depicts your desires in pictures is an outstanding tool. Regardless of your method, I suggest you schedule time on your calendar to review them in depth on at least a weekly basis. I like to visualize my Purposeful Vision each morning as a part of my daily meditation. I also review them in the written and picture form each week to truly anchor all the areas in my subconscious mind. During this time, I also evaluate where I am on my path of creation with these important aspects of my life and make course corrections where necessary. Above all, have fun with this process and enjoy how the presence of a Purposeful Vision can positively impact and guide your life.

2

BE THE CHANGE

Be the change you want to see in the world.
—Mahatma Gandhi

WE LIVE IN A "DOING" SOCIETY. FOR BETTER OR worse, how we see ourselves and how we are seen by others is predominantly based on what we do. Just think of our everyday conversations. When we meet someone for the first time, we say, "How do you *do*?" As the conversation progresses, we ask, "What do you *do* for a living?" When our children come home from school or our significant others or spouses come home from work, we ask, "What did you *do* today, honey?" So much of how we rate, evaluate and feel about ourselves is based on our doing: "Man, I got nothing *done* today" or "I feel great. I finally got that project *done!*"

Do, do, do—we are definitely a "doing" group of people. In fact, that mindset is what has brought so many of us the outstanding life successes we have experienced. We get things done. There is nothing wrong with doing for without it, we would never progress to the levels of our greatest potential.

However, a problem occurs when what we do or what we accomplish becomes our only way of identifying our value and the value of others. Our productivity becomes a measuring stick for our self-value and self-worth. As a result, we find ourselves literally becoming human "doings" versus human "beings."

If we are judging ourselves on what we are doing or not doing, there is a high probability we are also evaluating our happiness on what we have or do not have in our lives. Educational degrees, relationships, financial abundance and material possessions all become the standard for our overall success on this earthly plane. The more things we do, the more things we can have and the happier we will be.

The irony of this is that often the more we have, the more we feel we have to do to keep it. We con ourselves into believing that all this stuff is required for us to maintain our own happiness. It is as if "having-ness" has overtaken true happiness.

This is not to say that there is anything wrong with having beautiful things in our lives. A wonderful home, strong and vibrant relationships and material possessions can support our level of happiness. However, when they become the measuring stick for our overall self-concept, they can become a skewed part of a never-ending cycle of achieving and receiving—all in our effort to find happiness and security solely outside of ourselves.

Several years ago, I attended a personal development workshop where the facilitator of the event discussed these concepts. In a room full of successful, hardworking and high-achieving adults, his message rang true. He spoke of how most of us live our lives anchored in the belief that nothing is more important than what we do and what we have. He went on to say that he saw how this kind of thinking spun most of us into living our lives backward, subscribing to a life path that looks like this:

HAVE—DO—BE

The underlying thought process of this model goes something like this:

When I **have** enough money, then I will **do** the things I want to do, and then I will **be** happy.

When I **have** more time, then I will **do** the vacation with my family, and then I will **be** a better father/husband/mother/wife.

When I **have** more customers, then I will **do** the expansion of my business, and I will **be** successful.

When I **have** _____, then I will **do** _____, and then (and only then) I will **be** _____.

Is any of this hitting home? I know it did for me. I realized that so much of my self-worth and happiness were reliant on things outside of me, on the conditions that surrounded me and the reactions of those around me. I realized that even when I had obtained those things I thought would bring me joy, pride and excitement, I was actually still plagued with a feeling of discontent. I would inevitably begin searching, again and again, for that next thing that would undoubtedly bring me happiness. I realized I thought those outside conditions and material possessions would change what was going on inside of me; it was a way of being that I yearned for, but I was looking in all the wrong—places for it—outside of me.

During my talks, I often ask audiences, "Who would like more money in their lives?" Hands rocket into the air so quickly and forcefully, I often think people will dislocate their shoulders. I then ask them why they want more money. Some of the most common responses are: "So I can pay my bills," "So I can take care of my family's needs," "So I can give more away" and "So I don't have to worry about money."

After years of asking this question to audiences, what I have come to understand is that these folks who say they want more money are actually yearning for certain feelings they deem positive. They wish to experience themselves, and experience the world around them, as *being* more positive. Yes, the key word is "being"—they are yearning for a way of *being*. For example:

- Paying one's bills on time translates into *being responsible.*
- Taking care of one's needs translates into *being secure.*
- Giving more away to others translates into *being generous.*
- Relieving worries about money translates into *being free.*

Do we really need endless stacks of green paper with dead presidents stamped on them or bank accounts with large numbers in the ledger to make us feel any of these ways? In consciousness, NO! In reality, I am not saying that money is unimportant or that it can't help you get certain things for your life. Let's face it; we do live here, in the physical world, where money does have its importance. As motivational speaker Anthony Robbins says, "If you don't think money is important, you must be shopping somewhere else."

Truth be told, any of these states of being I listed (and many more) can be accessed through other means, means that have nothing to do with a dollar (euro, yen, etc.) sign. Regardless of the state of your personal or business finances, you could wake up in the morning and simply *choose* to think thoughts that feel secure, generous and free; you could choose to *act* in ways that made you feel secure, generous and free. Each one of these "ways of being" is actually something we create inside ourselves, independent of outside circumstances.

We have all heard of or know people who are considered wealthy by today's standards, yet they are not in a state of being happy, secure, generous or free. We know this because they're in legal battles to protect their stash or make more of it, or they have public addictions or family squabbles. On the other side of the coin (excuse the pun), we've heard stories of people with few belongings and no money to speak of who express great joy and serve others with generosity.

The truth in both situations is that money has nothing to do with the people. The real issue relates to that which is internal, not external. It is about the *way of being* each person carries within, their inner definition of self and their life that is the crucial part of the equation. If they feel they are rich inside, they express that in the world. If they feel poor inside, they cannot have enough outer wealth to change that. This is the meaning behind the adage, "You can't buy happiness."

Thankfully, for us, there is a happy ending to this story, a way out of living a "Have/Do/Be" life. The astute seminar facilitator, through his observations, saw that most successful and happy people have simply learned to rearrange these three simple words. The Have/Do/Be way of being was not their way of being. The key for them—and for any of us—is having the mindset of:

BE—DO—HAVE

If you want to be more loving, secure, courageous, confident, generous, trusting, peaceful, responsible or joyous, simply make the choice to **be** that way in your life. Then **do** the things in your life that support this way of being and you can **have** whatever it is you want. When I heard this, it was transformational for me. I realized that I could deliberately create my state of being, support it with powerful actions and as a result, experience the things in life that I wanted.

Let's look more closely at how this plays out in our lives. Simply stated, whatever is going on outside of us (lack of money, health problems, strained relationships, career struggles) has no intrinsic power. We, as the perceivers of those conditions and the reactors to them, do, however, give those outside stimuli certain powers. That's what we need to change. As my teachers at University of Santa Monica, Drs. Ron and Mary Hulnick, so astutely remind us, "How you deal with the issue inside yourself is the issue."

Have you ever had someone in your life whose behavior drove you nuts? Maybe it was a spouse who questioned you after a long day at work or your mother who constantly reminds you how you never call or an associate at work who loves to stop by your desk and talk incessantly. Perhaps their behavior brings so much agitation within you that it is difficult to be in the same room, much less carry on a conversation with them.

Although you might first believe that the other person is the cause of your upset, after some deep introspection using the Be/Do/Have model, you can come to realize that you actually have a choice in how you respond to their actions. Furthermore, you have a choice in how you perceive and interpret their actions. That choice *is* your responsibility—how do you want to be inside yourself in relating to them and others? What's your Purposeful Vision for relationships? Now you can choose to interpret these situations as perfect opportunities for self-development and choose to demonstrate higher degrees of patience with these people in your life. You may then set your sights on embodying the quality of patience in your life and commit yourself to enacting the most patient version—or vision—of yourself.

Here's a head's up: You may also soon realize that the setting of this intention, and your focused commitment to it, is not a magic wand that instantly transforms you into the epitome of patience. Frequently, you begin to see more occasions, or even extreme versions of these trying situations, showing up in your life. It is as if you have become a magnet for situations that give you "opportunities" to develop and demonstrate patience. So, in asking for more patience, the Universe brings you that one person or situation that completely tests your resolve for serenity, that petty tyrant that pushes all of your buttons.

This is where many people give up in frustration. This is also where you need to call on your *Inner Champion* to hold fast to your Purposeful Vision as you practice Being the Change you want to see so you can do your life differently and have the true patience you seek. As you practice patience inside you and in your actions, you begin showing a level of mastery in patience. That is when it seems like the magic wand comes into play. One day you notice, all those button-pushing people or situations seem to disappear or you notice the negative charge you felt toward them seems to vanish— "Abracadabra!" Once the lesson is learned, you don't need any more of those opportunities. It seems instantaneous but acknowledge yourself for the inner work that made it possible—you'll want to remember this model for life's next opportunities and lessons.

BEING THE CHANGE: ROB'S STORY

Rob, a student of mine and training partner, was one of those individuals that offered me many opportunities in mastering the quality of patience. The lessons he taught me extend into the level of life lessons and self-mastery around this quality of Being the Change, and I will be forever grateful to him for being in my life.

It had been a lifelong dream of mine to compete in and

win a national championship in Olympic Taekwondo. After college, I seriously considered the pursuit of this dream; however, my commitment to being a responsible and attentive husband and father took precedence over my dream. In 1998 when I was 35 years old, a national division opened up for competitors ages 33–40. Knowing that my athletic prime and my ability to compete against the younger competitors had most likely passed, the new division allowed me the chance to realize my dream.

In preparation for those competitions, I trained harder than I had for anything in my life. My hard work paid off, and I won the United States Taekwondo Union's National Championship in 1999.

An individual who turned out to be an integral person in my success was Rob. Rob was a tall, good-looking, athletic man in his late twenties. He had strong technical abilities, a driving spirit and the ability to take a shot. Rob became my main sparring partner as I prepared for my national matches.

Being a competitive athlete all of my life, I have noticed an interesting and somewhat amusing phenomenon. Those individuals with whom I competed the hardest, with whom I traded the fiercest blows, and from whom I received the greatest amount of punishment became the people with whom I created the closest bonds. Those training partners helped bring out the best in me through their constant challenging of my abilities. By consistently pushing me to the edge and forcing me to go beyond what I thought was possible, they were key contributors to my level of success. This process also proved to be a catalyst for uncovering my fears and short-comings, and the level of vulnerability I experienced clearly deepened my friendships.

As much as I loved Rob, he had one annoying habit. Each Tuesday and Thursday he would arrive at my martial arts school for our rigorous two-hour training session. Without fail, he would spend the first 15 to 20 minutes of our training session talking to me about everything that was going wrong in his life. So there I'd be, stretching, warming up and preparing for our session while Rob was off on the side of the mat, moving through his diatribe of despair. He complained about his work, he complained about his mother, he complained about his girlfriend, and he complained about traffic. The routine was always the same. It was as if someone put a quarter in him and he began spewing all of his life's troubles on cue.

At first I was interested in listening to him and being an attentive friend. I found myself getting caught up in the drama of what was happening in his life. At times I offered what I thought was productive coaching to handle the situations. Sometimes I found distorted pleasure in commiserating with him. Soon, though, this process got old, and I began to get irritated with this consistent dose of negative energy that threatened to overtake my training and focus on becoming a national champion.

One day, I finally had enough. As Rob went into another troubling life story, I said to him, "I've got it. I think I see the common denominator in all of your troubles." He stopped abruptly and looked at me as if I were bringing the tablets of truth down from the mountaintop. He excitedly asked, "What is it?"

I paused and delicately said to him, "Every time you have a problem at work, every time you have a problem with your girlfriend, every time you have a problem with your mother—*you* are there."

The statement clearly shocked him. After a moment of awkward silence, he tilted his head to one side and looked at me like a curious puppy seeing himself in the mirror for the first time. In the next moment, a look of "Aha, I got it!" lit up his face. He understood that each time he encountered turmoil and conflict in his relationships, he had an active part in that creation. In fact, as we discussed it further, he realized that in every situation, he was the one who was responsible. He created, promoted or allowed every one of those unwanted circumstances. How? By how he was *being*. When he was *being* impatient, it was mirrored back to him. When he was *being* frustrated, he got the same in return. When he was *being* judgmental of a person or situation, he soon felt that judgment directed right back at him. No wonder he was in such a quandary; he was chasing a tail of his own making without realizing it.

This was a sobering lesson for Rob, and when he began to understand the depth of this concept, he began to change and things began to change around him. His relationship with his boss at transformed into one of cooperation and respect. He and his girlfriend moved through their differences with grace and understanding, eventually moving into a closer relationship with one another. He was more patient and accepting as he was driving in traffic. These, as well as many other areas of his life, seemed to flow more smoothly.

What Rob learned is that by taking responsibility for his way of being, he could have a direct impact on how he perceived, interpreted and reacted to everyone and everything in his life. He learned, as author Dr. Wayne W. Dyer states, "When you change the way you look at things, the things you look at change."

So I ask you, what do you want more of in your life? Do you want more love, more peace, more joy? Do you want to live your life with more courage, confidence, patience? We're talking about the realm of the *Inner Champion* here. So, whatever you want to experience more of in your life, call on your *Inner Champion* and choose to **_be_** that way regardless of external circumstances. **_Be_** more loving, courageous, confident, trusting, peaceful, joyous. Then **_do_** the things that support that way of being, again regardless of what others do. You and your *Inner Champion* can then watch how those qualities you want to **_have_** in your life begin to manifest. What is consistent with the way in which you are *being* will begin to show up in your daily life. As you play with this concept in your day-to-day experiences, you will find yourself flowing closer and closer to mastering the Be/Do/Have lifestyle and moving further down your path to self-mastery. Let your *Inner Champion* be your guide, training partner, friend, and companion.

SHIFTING TO A BE/DO/HAVE MINDSET: JANICE'S STORY

I have found two exercises that help tap into our *Inner Champion* to alter the outdated Do/Have/Be patterns and transform ourselves into using the Be/Do/Have mindset to positively impact our lives. To demonstrate, let's follow a woman named Janice as she works her way through the process.

Janice had been with the same pharmaceutical company for more than ten years working as a district sales manager. Over the past several years, she had grown stagnant in her work and was looking for a change. Janice longed to work in a career that excited her and would fit better into her lifelong dreams. Six months prior, a career opportunity presented itself that was more consistent with the work she wanted to do in the world. However, she delayed pursuing the opportunity and the position went to someone else.

Still feeling her disappointment over the lost opportunity, Janice decided to learn from that situation to avoid any kind of a repeat performance. First, she reflected on how she had been thinking of herself and showing up in the world during the situation. She made a list of disempowering ways of being that contributed to the situation. With list in hand, she recalled the situation, looking for those ways of being that played key roles in the disappointing outcome. She realized her lack of action stemmed primarily from three disempowering ways of being. First, she was *fearful* of taking a leap. Although her current job was unfulfilling, it did offer her a sense of security she was too afraid to give up. Second, she saw she had been overly *cautious* in her approach, and as a result she had procrastinated in applying for the new position. Third, she was actually *uncommitted* to making a real change in her career. Upon further reflection, Janice noticed that these disempowering ways of being were not unique to this particular situation. In fact, they had plagued her throughout most of her life, creating a pattern of behavior and results.

After her self-reflection, Janice decided she clearly wanted to create a new expression of herself in the area of career. She wanted to work with a new company in an industry that fit perfectly with her interests. Janice had always enjoyed fitness and nutrition, and she had a keen interest in nutritional supplements that increase performance. She also was outgoing and loved to help people achieve their fitness goals. So Janice decided to pursue a job in sales, working for a company that specialized in dietary nutritionals.

Janice's next step was to realize that in order to actually move into the new career of her dreams, she needed to **_be_** the change she wanted to see to change some of her old patterns. She would no longer be demonstrating disempowerment. Janice was now focused on empowerment. She was choosing to *be* *committed* in her pursuit, making her job search a priority in her life. Janice also understood she needed to be *proactive* and choose to take steps every day toward finding her next career. Finally, Janice accepted that she would need to be *courageous*. She now chose to step out of her comfort zone armed with her awareness of being courageous. She chose to leave that old, secure job behind, as well as her fearful thoughts.

Janice asked herself the question, "What would I have to **_do_** to support my new way of being?" She made a new list of empowering ways of being, and from it she created a plan of action. Her list of actions were in alignment with being *committed, proactive* and *courageous* and served as her guide to the following steps she could easily take.

- Revise my résumé.
- Update my LinkedIn profile.
- Go online to research companies doing the type of work I am interested in doing and research what is currently going on in the market.
- Take a friend who is working in a similar field out to lunch and obtain insight into that industry.
- Call a corporate recruiter and discuss possible career opportunities.

Janice's final step was a key step for anyone who is truly focused on manifesting something new. She took the time to experience her new career and new way of being deep inside herself in a visceral way. She then wrote a detailed description of what her new career as a sales executive for a nutritional supplements company would look like. Much like chapters in a novel, these visions of her new career were vivid and exhilarating. She depicted everything: the environment and people she would encounter, the service she would provide, the salary she would make, the lifestyle she would be able to maintain, and most of all, what experience she would have inside of herself.

Clarity and Awareness Exercise

Now, it's your turn. Keep in mind you are looking for information to help you change, not for evidence of limitations.

1. As you sit quietly, reflect on a time in your life when things did not turn out as well as you had hoped. Maybe you lost your job, had a painful breakup or failed to reach one of your most sought after goals.

2. Allow yourself some time to take an honest inventory of how you were showing up in life during this time. What ways of *being* did you embrace or embody that could be identified as less than positive and empowering? In other words, if you missed the mark on creating something you wanted in your world, what were you experiencing that did not demonstrate you showing up at your best? Start with the following list.

Disempowering Ways of Being

Cautious	Confused	Cynical	Doubtful
Fearful	Frustrated	Hesitant	Pessimistic
Reserved	Resigned	Uncommitted	Unfocused

3.   After reviewing the list, once again reflect on your loss/pain/disappointment. You might see that much of this list describes how you were showing up. Or you might feel other words better describe your way of being in the past. Whatever thoughts and words come to you, take time to write them down on a piece of paper. Set your list aside as you read on and contemplate how this exercise can serve you.

Chances are that when you do a personal inventory, as Janice did, you will find you have some habitual ways of being that have prevented you from experiencing a more fulfilling life. Finding ourselves stuck in these patterns is common and a part of the human condition. So please be easy on yourself and refrain from any harsh judgments. Remember, the first step in creating change, in any area of your life, is awareness. From the point of awareness, you can consciously choose to embody new ways of being and choose to demonstrate those through congruent actions.

It is important to point out that the less than empowering ways of being, those that you displayed in the past, were merely coping strategies you created that were probably successful at the time. You (that former you) believed those strategies were the best you could do under those circumstances. Remember, back then you were dealing with a different (smaller picture) view of yourself and your options. You had not yet discovered your *Inner Champion*.

That being said, the present, wiser you can now choose new ways of being, embodying them in more empowering ways and create new strategies for success. There is no need to harbor any regret or guilt about the past. That was then, and this is now. By identifying and accepting those old disempowering ways of being, having a Purposeful Vision you want to fulfill and having your *Inner Champion* by your side, you can choose to break free from the old patterns. You now have the power to create a better present and a more successful and happy future. From this point, you now are ready for the second exercise.

Creating What You Want Exercise

1. Select one of the eight *areas of impact* of your life you would like to improve and/or change: career, relationships, health/wellness, financial, spiritual, service, leisure, and material things. You could choose the level of service you provide to your community or charitable organizations, for example, or something applying to an entire area, such as finding a love relationship. You get to decide. Take some time to look at all of the areas and determine one where you would most like to make a positive impact in your life.

2. After you have determined which area of impact you would like to change, think about what you would like to see

in this area. Use the space provided to write down your vision as an intention. Be as descriptive as possible, noting the "who, what, where and why" of the scene you are choosing to create. As you visualize, use colorful imagination and specific scenarios. See yourself being that empowered individual in whatever area of impact you have chosen. Have fun!

_____

_____

_____

_____

3. Once you've fleshed out your vision of your area of personal expansion, ask yourself the following question. "To get want I want in this area of my life, *how would I have to be* in this situation?" The list below provides some possible examples.

Empowering Ways of Being

Accepting Adventurous Committed   Enthusiastic
Expressive Focused   Open-Minded Passionate
Proactive   Relaxed   Reliable   Responsible

Once again, do not be limited by this list. Rather, choose whatever comes to mind. Embrace the word(s) that speak to you, whether from this page or from your *Inner Champion*. Know that as you are pondering this question, you are beginning a powerful creative process. The list will act as a positive catalyst in moving you toward the life experience you want. Using Janice's process as a model, identify the ways of being you will need to embrace to make your intention a reality. Think of the times you felt most in alignment with your Self and felt the most empowered. How were you being? Write those qualities here:

_____

_____

_____

_____

_____

4. With those qualities in mind, ask the question, *What would I have to **do** to support my new way of being?* In other words, what are some of those actions I need to take that would move me closer to attaining my goal? As you answer this question, you will begin to see your next steps emerge. You might see an entire plan, but that is not necessary. Your next step will emerge and the next step after that as you keep your vision and ways of being in mind and take the steps that emerge.

_____

_____

_____

_____

5. Complete this process by asking yourself the question, *"What would I **have** if I got want I wanted?* Please allow yourself time to get clear about what you want things to look like. Allow yourself to dream, letting your imagination take

you to where your heart wants to go. Give yourself permission to embody this so deeply that you begin to feel the sensations of living that success. How does your body feel? How does your heart feel? Allow this to become a visceral experience as you are detailing what this new area of your life will be like. When you feel it all with you, write a picturesque scene, one in which you are living your preferred life experience.

_____

_____

_____

_____

_____

_____

_____

_____

There you have it. A simple and effective way of creating the Be/Do/Have mindset and using its power to manifest the life experiences you want. I have used this process in my own life as well as with my clients. It is a potent tool for getting clear, becoming empowered and moving through the unknown into a new venture. I once had a life-coach client express it this way, "Hanging out in the known, even if it is far from the desired life experience, is all too common. It is natural to fear the unknown and resolve oneself to the shackles of predictability." However, by focusing on the being-ness first, you call forth your *Inner Champion* and allow yourself the gift of greater clarity and enhanced strength of heart. You ensure that the changes you make are created on the inside first, which is always the most important part of transformation.

Give it a try and remember to *be the change* you want to see and have in your life.

3

INTEGRITY

Integrity is telling myself the truth.
And honesty is telling the truth to other people.
—Spencer Johnson

INTEGRITY—WHAT AN INTERESTING WORD. WHEN I speak with audience members and clients about integrity and what it means to them in their lives, the responses I receive generally fall into the following categories.

- honesty
- holding strong to your values
- doing what you say you will do
- doing the right thing

What I find interesting is that these responses generally speak of how we relate to others in the world and how we carry ourselves in relationship to others. Although I find this to be extremely important, as a Quality of Black Belt Leadership, means integrity toward one's Self and how, from that launching point, we can show up powerfully and effectively in the world.

In martial arts, the quality of integrity plays an instrumental role in the character development of its practitioners. In fact, in the martial art of Tae Kwon Do, integrity, along with courtesy, perseverance, self-control and indomitable spirit stand as pillars in the development of students' character. These codes of behavior are required not only in the martial arts classroom but more important, in everyday life.

In his landmark book *Taekwon-Do: The Korean Art of Self-Defense*, known to many as the bible of Tae Kwon Do, the art's founder, Gen. Choi Hong Hi, defines integrity as follows:

In Tae Kwon Do, the word integrity assumes a much looser definition than the one usually presented in Webster's dictionary. One must be able to define right and wrong, and have a conscience, if wrong, to feel guilt.

Gen. Choi goes on to articulate that embracing integrity in this way is demonstrated by instructors and students of Tae Kwon Do by staying true to the quality of martial arts techniques they teach, avoiding the attainment of martial arts ranks for egotistical purposes or promoting their martial arts solely for materialistic gains.

The primary definition in the Merriam-Webster dictionary states integrity is "the firm adherence to a code of especially moral or artistic values: INCORRUPTIBILITY."

Although I subscribe to these definitions, I believe integrity has a much more expansive definition that needs to be understood not only for one to be an effective student of martial arts but of life as well. For those choosing the path toward Self-understanding, I believe it is vital to have a solid comprehension of how true integrity starts from within.

In his article, "Integrity: Without It Nothing Works," printed in *Rotman Management*, the magazine of the Rotman School of Management in Toronto, Harvard University's Michael C. Jensen defines integrity as "A state or condition of being whole, complete, unbroken, unimpaired, sound, in perfect condition."

Take, for instance, the chair you are sitting on. Because

of its state of wholeness and soundness, as demonstrated by its four sturdy legs, strong back and stable seat, you are able to sit with confidence in its ability to support you as you read these words. If you are in your home, the walls are in integrity as they maintain their structure and support the roof overhead. If they were not, the structure would collapse upon itself.

The same holds true for us and our word. When we are true to ourselves and others in our communications, commitments and actions, we find ourselves in a state of completeness and wholeness that allows us to experience congruency with who we really are. When this congruency exists, we are in our power, with a clear focus, in the flow of life. On the other hand, when our words and actions are incongruent with our inner truth, we can find ourselves imbalanced, distracted and working against the flow of life. Life can become difficult, not because of the challenges that necessarily exist in our outside world, but because we experience ourselves in an inner state of turmoil and struggle.

We live in a world that can be extremely demanding, pulling us in a multitude of directions. Our inner struggle can become increasingly challenging at these times, despite our best intentions, when we are so "busy" we are unable to fulfill the agreements and commitments we have made to ourselves and others.

But busy-ness is often looked upon as a prerequisite of being productive and dependable. I remember hearing several times as a young man, "If you want anything done, give it to a busy person." This statement reinforces the fact society honors busy-ness. People often wear their busy-ness as a sort of badge. "Oh, I am so busy," "Man, I have a lot going on," "Sorry I did not return your call; I have been very busy." Busy-ness has become an accepted way of living; what's more, if we are not busy, we often feel as if others look upon us as lazy, lost or inadequate.

Please understand—there is nothing wrong with busy-ness, but I am making the distinction between being busy and being productive. Being productive allows us to be the fullest expression of who we are. Being busy does not necessarily mean that we are productive or on course with our life purpose. In fact, busy-ness can sometimes be the greatest vehicle we use for avoiding what it is that most needs to be done for us to live our true purpose. As author and super-coach Steve Chandler writes, "Busy-ness is the surest form of laziness."

Think about it. Have you ever had a day when you were busy all day but got nothing done? Of course we all have. Those types of days are often filled with minor tasks such as responding to email, running errands or commuting to and from jobs, meetings, events. How do those days make you feel? If you are like me, you feel frustrated and confused, asking yourself how you can be so busy but not seem to move forward. It is like being on the proverbial hamster wheel and wondering, "Will I ever get off?" or "How will I ever get ahead?"

This kind of frustration usually is heightened when we fail to focus on what we have defined as the most important parts of our lives, such as devoting time to our life purpose or spending time on the relationships we feel are most important to us. In essence, we have broken an agreement with ourselves or others, and this causes an incongruence inside of us. This deep feeling of incongruence, these broken promises to oneself or others, can result in an entanglement of guilt and frustration. When I find myself in this state, I feel overwhelmed and the energy drains from me.

It is as if an energetic cord littered with unfulfilled commitments exists between the present moment and the past, so that I sense I am dragging the past with me into the future. Even if the promises or commitments do not exist in my conscious mind, they clearly reside in my subconscious. If I have not done my work to effectively complete or release these commitments, I find myself expending energy I am not even consciously aware is being displaced.

In their outstanding book, *Conscious Loving*, authors Gay and Kathlyn Hendricks have this to say about the impact of breaking our agreements in our relationships:

> *Each broken agreement leaches energy from within us and in the relationship itself. Energy in a relationship depends on a fairly delicate communication. Break an agreement and you drop a brick on this fragile structure you have built. In close relationships it does not matter whether an agreement is big or little: break one and it lessens aliveness.*

I have a much different experience when I do what I say I will. In keeping my word I enjoy the steady and free-flowing surge of energy that is the by-product of being congruent with my integrity. Life seems to flow, and I have what feels like a limitless amount of energy to help propel me through my day. In keeping my commitments, I draw on my *Inner Champion* and feel refreshed, energized and seated in my power as I move from situation to situation and project to project.

It is important here to make a distinction between what business author Michael C. Jensen says is the difference between "keeping" our word and "honoring" our word. In *keeping* our word, we always do what we say we will in the timing we committed for it to be completed—from completing a project in a timely manner at work to picking up the dry cleaning you promised your wife you would or staying consistent with your daily walks around the block.

This is not always easy to do. You might be sitting there reading this book feeling strongly about keeping your word, but recognizing you are a busy person and sometimes things fall through the cracks. Sometimes life just happens and there is nothing that can be done to change the circumstances we face. What then? This is where *honoring* our word comes into play and expands the idea of personal integrity.

We might not have control over the circumstances that arise, but we do have control over the way we choose to respond. What we commit to is keeping our word in all possible cases and honoring our word in one of two ways when we can't. 1) We renegotiate our commitments in advance when we see issues coming. This means taking the time to directly gain agreement between ourselves and the other party to change dates, times or other elements of what we committed to for the best possible outcome. 2) We also pro-actively take steps if we are unable to meet our commitments to address what needs to be done as soon as it can be done. This means we take 100 percent responsibility to complete our commitment in the best way possible for all concerned. We also take proactive steps for the future that will move us closer to preventing these occurrences.

Honoring our word is finding the balance between keeping our word to the best of our ability as often as we can and making good on our word when circumstances surface so we maintain the integrity needed to form trusting relationships and improve our life experience.

THE POWER OF KEEPING AGREEMENTS

Several years ago, I immersed myself in transformational leadership training for a month. My fifteen fellow participants, like me, had a deep desire to achieve greater levels of mastery in their personal and professional lives. On the first day, the facilitator began a talk on the power and impor-tance of successfully following through on the commitments we made to ourselves and others. I think I can speak for our group of both intelligent and conscious individuals when I say we collectively thought we had these issues under con-trol. Each of us prided ourselves in living a life of integrity and keeping our word. The facilitator then presented us with a challenging assignment.

He stated that for the next 28 days, as a means of becoming aware of the power of our agreements, whenever we broke a commitment with others or ourselves, we were to fill out a one-page report recognizing this, detailing the circumstances, and stating what we would do to correct the situation by taking 100 percent responsibility for its creation. An uncomfortable murmur began to build in the group as we noted the directions did not relate just to large issues or projects with which we were engaged but also the little things we often unconsciously dismiss.

For instance, if we said we would meet someone for lunch at noon and we showed up at 12:03 p.m., we had broken an agreement. If we promised ourselves we would get up at 6 a.m. to run before our morning session, but the pillow called our name until 7, we had broken an agreement. If we committed ourselves to being careful with our diets but reached for that dessert—agreement broken.

The group's murmur built to an agitated frenzy when people began to understand the scope of this assignment. The question was raised, "But wait a minute here; we are extremely busy people and you have to cut us some slack. We are putting in twelve- to fourteen-hour days as part of this seminar, and we can't truly be expected to keep our word or agreements in *all* instances, can we?"

The answer quickly came back, "You can—and you will."

I reacted with frustration and anger in my belief that my integrity was being challenged in this assignment. I then remembered that when something irritates, frustrates or angers me, it is usually something I need to take a closer look at. I further realized what I had considered little things would be where I found the greatest opportunity for improvement. As my cumulative number of instances of poor follow-through on the little things began to mount, I saw their potential to become just as disruptive or even more unbalancing than missing the mark on what I considered to be an important agreement.

My feelings of frustration and anger while living through the conscious experience of failing and judging myself for not being able to keep my word eventually transformed into feelings of humility and acceptance of myself and others. Another lesson I learned was I needed a tool to better deal with my level of completion of agreed-to tasks.

THE 5 D'S OF KEEPING AGREEMENTS

It was from this experience that I formulated a five-step process for staying in my integrity and proactively dealing with my commitments. I call it the "5 D's of Keeping Agreements." As I said when we took our personal inventory, the first step in healing or changing a habit or behavior that no longer serves us is awareness. This process is designed to bring awareness to the challenges that might come present when we feel we are inundated with commitments or are developing a pattern of falling short on our agreements to ourselves and others.

As with any process, I encourage you to be as honest and forthcoming in your responses as possible to gain the true benefit of this exercise. Again, be cautious about negatively judging yourself or your circumstances. Labeling yourself as "wrong" or "irresponsible" has the tendency to deplete rather than increase our energy and resources. We want to free up our energy so we can show up in the most powerful and effective way possible, not berate ourselves for the ineffective methods of the past.

This is another job for your *Inner Champion*, the part of you that truly has all the answers you are looking for. Find a time when you can be alone for 20 to 30 minutes of uninterrupted time. Close the door, turn off the TV or computer, put your cell phone on silent and commit yourself to taking an honest look into your life around this issue.

The First D: Detail It. Take out a piece of paper and list everything you have committed to do in your current life. This means EVERYTHING! Take a look at your family commitments, your professional or job-related projects, your health and wellness goals, any service projects for organizations you belong to or services you provide at your place of worship. I find it most helpful to divide the committed tasks into the four key areas of Career, Family/Relationships, Health/Wellness and Home/Service Responsibilities. Your list may look something like this:

Career
- Complete monthly P/L report
- Meet with Dave to determine next project staffing

- Deliver talk to Rotary Club
- Meet Greg for lunch
- Complete MS Outlook training
- Train staff on telephone skills
- Complete staff performance reviews
- Call new clients to set up intro meetings
- Reserve conference room for Friday's meeting
- Complete October/November/December shipping estimates

Family/Relationships
- Coach Jimmy's soccer team three days a week
- Date night with wife
- Take Lindsay to orthodontist
- Call Mom to set up holiday (Thanksgiving/ Christmas) plans
- Call brother to set up fall hunting trip

Health/Wellness
- Work out at gym (Mon/Wed/Fri)
- Run 5K race
- Go to yoga class two times per week
- Schedule annual physical
- Meditate daily
- Lose 10 pounds
- Make appointments with nutritionist to analyze diet

Home/Service Responsibilities
- Clean basement
- Fix gate on fence
- Mail in quarterly taxes
- Cut the lawn
- Get the oil changed in car
- Participate in a food drive
- Complete reading three books on nightstand
- Follow up on emails to perspective clients
- Fix faucet at Grandma's house
- Call Comcast to upgrade home cable

The Second D: Delete It. The next step is to take out a red pen and delete everything you are choosing *not* to do at this time. Often this takes extreme courage as we ask ourselves to let go of things we feel we have to do. But take a close look at your items and decide if they really need to be done at this time. Would your world fall apart if the fence gate is not fixed now? Can you renegotiate that lunch with a work associate? Be selective about the items you know need to be done and eliminate the things from your list that can be let go of or rescheduled until another time. Often we choose to think that everything is a priority, but when we hold that belief, nothing is a priority and we disperse our energies in all directions, continually draining ourselves of our precious internal resources—and building up mistrust in ourselves to do what we say we will do.

The Third D: Defer It. You might also feel concern that particular items need to be done at sometime in the future, so how can you delete them from your list? What if you forget to complete this task and create more work in the long run? For those items you choose to take off your list but need your attention in the future defer them. Create a "Suspended Action" file or a "Someday, Maybe List." Place these items in the file and commit to reviewing this list monthly. It may be a physical file or part of your computer's integrated management calendar system. If the item requires your attention next month, place it back on your list. Remove it if it no longer seems relevant for you.

The Fourth D: Delegate It. If you are like me, this might be the most difficult step. As you know, no one can do something better than you can (smile). When I first opened my martial arts school, I did it all. I taught all of the classes, answered the phone, took the appointments, did the introductory lessons, enrolled new students, renewed their student membership programs, and mopped the floor and took out the garbage.

All was going well until I reached the 100-student plateau. I stayed there for several months and could not move beyond this threshold. I was tapped out in my capacity to serve my students and family, and I grew more and more frustrated as I could not grow my school beyond that level to the place I desired. I finally discovered I needed to delegate responsibilities and adequately train others to do the tasks I was doing.

Look at it this way. Let's assume we have a finite amount of energy (say, 100 units) to put forth in our work and lives. Once we reach this threshold, we are unable to expand any further because units of energy allocated have been tapped.

If we have 10 tasks, we might be able to put only 10 percent of our effort into each task. However, if we train someone to do the same tasks, even if they are not as proficient as we were when we had our total energy invested in the job, their total attention to the work is likely to be better than our partial commitment to the task. Let's say they were at best 50 percent of our best capacity; their 50 percent is better than the 10 percent attention we could give to the work.

Reflect also on the times someone had faith in you and guided you in the process of expansion by appropriately and consciously providing you with greater responsibilities. How did that make you feel? How did someone having confidence and faith in you positively impact how you developed as a self-assured, effective performer in the workplace? By delegating, we not only provide ourselves the break we need to focus on what is most important, but we also give our business or life the opportunity to expand while positively impacting someone else's growth and development.

The Fifth D: Do It. Now it is time to make things happen. By following the previous steps, your list of agreements is pared down and you can focus your time, energy and attention on the true priorities in your life. By releasing the uncompleted actions that serve as energy drains in the form of unfulfilled commitments, you have clearly identified key items and tasks to focus on, better ensuring they are done in a timely fashion with your full attention and energy. As you keep your agreements, you build congruence with your integrity and experience more joy in your life.

4

CONSCIOUS PERSISTENCE

Nothing in this world can take the place of persistence.
Talent will not; nothing is more common than unsuccessful
people with talent. Genius will not; unrewarded genius is almost
a proverb. Education will not; the world is full of educated
derelicts. Persistence and determination alone are omnipotent.
The slogan "press on" has solved and always will solve
the problems of the human race.
—Calvin Coolidge, 30th president
of the United States

PERSISTENCE IS A QUALITY POSSESSED BY history's greatest men and women and is the linchpin in overcoming challenges and hardships in order to make real change in the world. When we reflect on the lives of Gandhi, Martin Luther King Jr. and Nelson Mandela, who challenged popular beliefs and the status quo to transform nations, we see how their strength and persistence, made conscious through purposeful vision, created lasting change in our world.

The rewards of conscious persistence are not saved for those who are immortalized in history. Each day, we can read stories or watch news reports of those who have overcome obstacles through persistence and realize their dreams or transform their lives. Hearing these stories reminds us on a deep level that the power to be victorious in our lives is present inside each of us. We can draw on our *Inner Champion* to supply the conscious persistence we need.

In martial arts, we have a saying, "A Black Belt is a White Belt that never quit." Given my years of teaching, I definitely stand behind the truth of this statement. In fact, rarely have I witnessed the most physically skilled beginners becoming the students who make it to Black Belt. These people often get bored and move on to the next athletic endeavor and next physical challenge. Conversely, most of those who eventually attain the prestigious rank of Black Belt are those who have struggled, physically, mentally or emotionally in their training. However, through their conscious persistence, they experience a breakthrough that helps them gain proficiency in their new art. Their persistent effort galvanizes their ability to break through obstacles and experience success—then yearn for greater learning, growth and expansion.

The dictionary defines one who is persistent as someone who "refuses to give up or let go" or who is "insistently repetitive or continuous." It could be argued that all of us are persistent in our lives. We maintain our schedules, we go to work each day at the same time we most likely drive the same route and put in the same hours each day. We are continuous in our diets, as we eat and drink the same things each week, regardless of their nutritional value. We repeat the same healthy or unhealthy patterns in our relationships, thinking someone else will have to change to fit us.

You see, all of us show signs of persistence, but are we doing so in ways that best serve us and the people around us? In many ways, the routines we have developed and the ways of being we have created are unconscious. We continue to express the same ways of being and the same ways of showing up, but we wonder why our lives remain the same. This unconsciousness is a choice, but sometimes it is so well hidden a lifetime can pass before we realize what we are doing.

It is for this reason that I urge you to take a step back and consider the power of consciously directing the quality of persistence in your life. What are the ways you are currently showing up that have become unconscious habits? What can you change, even in small ways, to help create more of what you want in your life? Where in your life are you willing to apply persistent effort to make a change?

CONSCIOUS PERSISTENCE: GEORGE'S STORY

George is an accountant for a large company. His life is good. He enjoys his work and his fellow employees and boss; he has a wonderful wife and two great kids. However, George has known for a long time that he needs to do something about his health. Now in his early forties, his last annual physical showed he is about 30 pounds overweight and his blood pressure is moving toward the unhealthy range. George does little to no physical exercise. With each new year comes the promise of getting to the gym, but life seems to continually get in the way and soon he finds himself in the same pattern of inactivity. George's father underwent heart surgery in his late forties and George has always wanted to avoid his father's fate, but he appears to be on the same path.

Another new year arrived, and George was committed to making a change in his life. This time, through work with a coach, he decided to take a good look at his lifestyle before embarking on his new exercise program. He realized that the changes he needed to make were not just behavioral; he needed to alter his thoughts and feelings on the inside. George took some time to examine the unconscious habits he had developed that had brought him to this point. Not doing so would simply set him up for failure as he slipped back into his old, unconscious habits.

George first looked at his morning routine. He usually got up at 6 each morning but then hit the snooze button two or three times before finally getting out of bed. He told himself he deserved the extra rest because of the hard work he put into his job. Once he was up, he was usually running late, with no time for breakfast other than a cup of coffee and a bagel or donut on the way out the door. George usually ate lunch on the go between appointments. By the time he got home at night, he was exhausted and wanted to do nothing but eat dinner and relax in front of the television.

Although George understood he was not happy with the results of his long-held routine, he continued with it because it had become so familiar he did not even think about it. He was persistent in its execution, doing the same thing, day in and day out, but he did so in an unconscious way. In looking at his habits, he began to understand he had simply been sleepwalking through life. He also realized that if he wanted to make changes, he would have to make conscious choices.

With the help of his coach, George developed a new nutrition plan and exercise routine. He committed to consistently follow his new regimen, knowing he would need conscious persistence over time to net him the positive changes he sought.

DISCIPLINE LEADS TO FREEDOM

And paradoxically, the more disciplined (warrior-like) I am with my actions, and with my precious time, the more disciplined I am in who I choose to communicate with and where I choose to guide those 40,000 thoughts each day. The more disciplined I become, the more free I am to have the life I want. If I conduct myself in a disciplined and organized way, I have much more free time.
—Steve Chandler, *Time Warrior*

Conscious persistence relies on discipline and freedom, which, at first glance, might appear to be diametrically opposed ways of being. When one thinks of discipline, images of austere rules, rigid schedules and harsh punishment might come to mind. Conversely, the idea of freedom evokes images of complete lack of responsibility and the ability to do as one pleases without consequences imposed by authority.

From the time we are children to well into our advanced stages of adulthood, there is an internal yearning to do as one pleases and not be subjected to the will of others by way of institutions of learning, our parents, our employers or even our significant others and spouses. Here again lies the misperception that freedom comes from an experience outside ourselves.

Freedom, however, is something we experience from the inside out. As Viktor Frankl wrote in his acclaimed book *Man's Search for Meaning* about his experience of surviving the Nazi concentration camps of World War II: "The one thing you can't take away from me is the way I choose to respond to what you do to me. The last of one's freedoms is to choose one's attitude in any given circumstance."

In taking a closer look at freedom and discipline, we see that freedom is supported by a framework of discipline we create in our lives. This synergy is revealed in their definitions:

Discipline: training that corrects, molds or perfects mental faculties or moral character; orderly or prescribed conduct or path of behavior

Freedom: the condition of being free; the power to act or speak or think without externally imposed restraints

When I first opened my martial arts school, I noticed an interesting phenomenon as summer vacation approached for my students. The anticipation of freedom from the routine of getting up early, going to school each day and doing homework was palpable in the martial arts classroom. Children smiled from ear to ear as they entered the studio and most could recite without hesitation how many days of school they had left.

You might think the exuberance the kids had expressed before school let out would sustain them for the summer. However, for many, the excitement they anticipated lasted only a week or two after school's actual dismissal.

Soon after the summer vacation honeymoon ended, one group of kids complained about being bored and having nothing to do. Their body language changed as they entered the martial arts studio, and it was more challenging to teach and motivate them. These children had no structure to their days. They were "free" to wake up when they wanted, eat whenever or whatever they wanted, do whatever they wanted to do.

Another group of kids maintained a degree of structure in their daily schedules. They woke up at regular times, maintained a healthy diet and participated in parent-planned activities each day. By having a disciplined way of living, these kids felt in balance and gained the most enjoyment from their summer vacation experiences.

This phenomenon does not stop at childhood but carries into our adult lives. Think about times you were in a routine and how it helped your life move and flow. The structure gave you the freedom to explore new ideas and opportunities from a position of strength and empowerment based on the consistency of your daily, weekly and monthly disciplines.

Take money and finances. Have you ever noticed that those who are "disciplined" with their money and spend mainly on necessities, invest for the future, and give regularly to charities also have the freedom to make purchases for things they desire when the opportunity arises? On the other hand, those who are "undisciplined" in the management of their money are rarely, if ever, free from the grip of financial problems, regardless of the amount they make in their professional lives.

The history of state lotteries is full of people who struggled financially prior to winning the jackpot. Although euphoric and full of hope when they received their winnings, the same sadness, frustration and despair regarding money they had prior to their big win resurfaced. Many found themselves penniless in months following their rise to millionaire-hood. The number of zeroes in their prize had nothing to do with their happiness but everything to do with their discipline in managing money. Their internal belief system about worthiness destroyed any sense of discipline regarding it and they experienced abandon but no internal freedom.

FREEDOM LEADS TO EXPANSION

As the quote below eloquently illustrates, it is almost never outside influences that keep us from our greatest expression of Self but our own limiting thought and beliefs about who we are.

Our deepest fear is not that we are inadequate. Our deepest fear is that we are powerful beyond measure. It is our light, not our darkness that most frightens us. We ask ourselves, Who am I to be brilliant, gorgeous, talented, fabulous? Actually, who are you not to be? You are a child of God. Your playing small does not serve the world. There is nothing enlightened about shrinking so that other people won't feel insecure around you. We are all meant to shine, as children do. We were born to make manifest the glory of God that is within us. It's not just in some of us; it's in everyone. And as we let our own light shine, we unconsciously give other people permission to do the same. As we are liberated from our own fear, our presence automatically liberates others.

——Marianne Williamson, *Return to Love*

In one of my all-time favorite quotes, Marianne Williamson urges us to accept and embrace the amazing power that exists within each one of us. When she poses the question, who are we *not* to be brilliant, gorgeous, talented and fabulous, she is really asking her readers to embrace the parts of themselves that for many are never realized. Discipline supports our freedom to overcome our fears and explore greater and more expansive ways for us to show up in the world.

The embracing of our individual greatness is paramount in building our personal belief in and acceptance of Self. More important, it is the only way we can truly, powerfully support and encourage others to share their individual gifts with the world. Nelson Mandela used Williamson's quote during his presidential inaugural address as he looked to unify 42 million South African citizens who had been divided and torn apart by decades of oppression from governmental apartheid.

Our world is in a constant state of change and expansion. Nature is a good example. Seasons change from the warmth of summer to the coolness of fall. Autumn moves into the coldness of winter. The dormant state of winter is transformed into the aliveness of spring. It happens naturally with such amazing precision that it can overwhelm our ability to understand how all of the magnitude takes place—particularly when we sometimes have difficulty just managing our everyday schedules or balancing our checkbooks. The key is that nature does not think about what it is doing. It doesn't question whether it is good enough, smart enough, wealthy enough, good-looking enough; it just does what it does, naturally. It doesn't have to worry if it has the correct amount of resources or when is the right time to move; it just moves.

Who are *you* not to be brilliant, gorgeous, talented and fabulous? Who is not giving you permission to do so? Sadly, the person most likely standing in your way is YOU!

Throughout my life, I have noticed that when I come upon the greatest obstacles to my growth, expansion and upliftment, those obstacles did not exist outside of me, but were a result of my own limiting thoughts and beliefs.

During my 35 years of teaching martial arts, I have seen thousands of students move through their own obstacles and self-doubt to achieve things in their martial arts training they never thought possible. I would state that the reason the attainment of Black Belt is so powerful is that there are few voluntary endeavors in this world that can challenge a person to look as deeply into themselves on a physical, mental, emotional and spiritual level than the journey to Black Belt. It, too, is the right blend of discipline and freedom that leads to expansion.

TRAVELING THE ROAD TO BLACK BELT

It is important to note that the road to Black Belt is not an easy one. For a student to even be considered for a 1st Degree Black Belt in my system of Tae Kwon Do, they must undergo at least three to three-and-a-half years of dedicated training. Once this time is completed, students who also meet the established criteria of physical and character proficiency are invited to participate in the Black Belt candidacy program. This program is a challenging sixteen-week period that requires students to participate in an intense physical curriculum. For example, in the four months leading up to Black Belt testing, in addition to participating in the normal activities of their regular martial arts classes, students must complete a minimum of 4,000 push-ups, 4,000 abdominal crunches, 4,000 kicking techniques, and 400 repetitions of their forms (katas); they also must run 40 miles, perform a specific maneuver 1,000 times to demonstrate perseverance, perform various self-defense techniques 160 times and spar a minimum of 120 rounds.

These requirements are the same whether a student is a 10-year-old boy looking to achieve his junior Black Belt or a 50-year-old woman looking to achieve her 1st Dan (Degree) ranking. The numbers might seem daunting, but it is here that the concept of conscious persistence is put into practice. I often remind students as they embark on this journey that when people are presented with any comprehensive life challenge, results rarely manifest instantly but are achieved through consistent daily practice.

To demonstrate this concept, I pose the simple question, "How do you eat an elephant?" After some confused and quizzical looks, I reveal to them that the only way to consume the enormous pachyderm is to do it "one bite at a time." I stress that any grand accomplishment or life transformation is achieved by taking consistent action toward a goal. In this way, 4,000 push-ups become 40 push-ups per day, six days per week for sixteen weeks. Forty miles of running become running approximately a mile per day, three days per week for a little more than four months. In following this formula for success, students achieve physical results never thought possible by consistent effort, plus they absorb a life-long lesson in the power of conscious persistence.

EXPANDING YOUR COMFORT ZONE

When I use the words "comfort zone," I am not talking simply about the enjoyment of everyday luxuries. When I come home at night and rest into my recliner with a good book and a fire going, or I curl up with a blanket on the couch with my sweetie to watch a movie, I am definitely enjoying comforts that I believe can be wonderful creations of self-nurturance.

The comfort zones I am referring to here are the situations or ways of being in our lives we have created that have become detrimental to our growth and expansion. Deciding to stay for extended periods of time in these states or life circumstances and avoiding moving into situations that can bring us opportunities for growth become opposing forces to our individual expression and empowerment. It is not uncommon for us to stay in unhappy situations like jobs, relationships or living conditions. We hold ourselves back by thoughts of limitations or aversion to moving into new areas. Rather than move into more powerful and expressive ways of being and living, we stay where we are because conditions feel familiar and safe, even when we know they are detrimental to our growth and happiness.

These situations give us a certain comfort and form the basis of our "stories," which represent struggle and strife and from whose grasp and depths we cannot find a way to release ourselves. When these stories solidify into our identity, their unhappiness and discomfort show up in how we communicate and connect with the world. This "woundology," a term coined by spiritual teacher and author Caroline Myss, becomes the pervasive belief system in our lives and is woven into the fabric of our relationships.

Recently, my good friend Brian O'Malley shared with me a key piece of wisdom he received from his beloved father. He said, "If you don't want to do something, don't do it. But if you aren't doing something because it scares you, do it." Brian has climbed Mount Everest on five different occasions. He has definitely learned how to move out of his comfort zone.

Instead of being an obstacle, fear should be our signal to take action. The action to move through our fears might be terrifying at first, but it is essential in breaking through to greater levels of happiness and Self-expression. The powers of the Universe meet us at the point of action. Or as philosopher Ralph Waldo Emerson stated, "Do the thing you fear, and the death of fear is certain." Your *Inner Champion* and your Conscious Persistence will see you through.

FOUR STAGES OF EXPANSION

As a martial arts practitioner, instructor and coach, I have observed four distinct stages of transformation that people, regardless of age, gender or ethnicity, move through as they expand their comfort zone in their ways of being, learning and operating in the world. These stages, inspired by Gordon Training International's *Four Stages of Learning a New Skill,* are not limited to business or career, but actually can be found in any area where we are being expanded when learning a new task or concept. You might recognize yourself or others in one or more of them. Take heart and let your awareness be a catalyst for calling forth your *Inner Champion* to help you more gracefully and consciously move through the stages toward a more impactful and powerful expansion.

Stage 1: Unconscious Incompetence. *You don't know what you don't know and you, therefore, have not yet developed a skill for it.*

Remember the last time you were challenged to learn something new? Remember the feelings of both nervousness and exhilaration that accompanied this process? Some of the most enjoyable times I have had in martial arts teaching occurred when I instructed students who had no frame of reference for a technique or new skill. Watching their eyes light up and their body physiology change as they began to learn to move their body in a whole new way is one of the greatest gifts I received as a teacher.

At the beginning stages of martial arts training, a student wears a White Belt. This stands for the purity of the new-fallen snow, with no previous training in the martial arts. It is often said that this is the most important belt of all, as this is the time when a practitioner comes to their training with an open mind and heart, waiting to receive the teaching that can lead to physical, mental and spiritual transformation. In many ways, the White Belt "doesn't know what they don't know" and they accept it. They expect to be a novice and with that, their minds and hearts are open and ready to learn. Knowing that they will be exposed to many things they do not have an experience and understanding of is part of the journey's excitement. The White Belt has undertaken the first step on their voyage, knowing that the only way they have to go is "up" in their learning and experience.

This is a first step of a natural progression of growth and awareness and it begins with total newness and unfamiliarity for the student. The unfamiliar then transforms into the familiar when the understanding of the new skill begins to take hold in the student's awareness. The final stage is when familiarity can eventually lead to mastery as skills are fully integrated in the student's body, mind and spirit. The late great martial arts icon Bruce Lee addressed the progression of these stages when he stated, *"Before I learned the art, a punch was just a punch, and a kick, just a kick. After I learned the art, a punch was no longer a punch, a kick, no longer a kick. Now that I* understand *the art, a punch is just a punch and a kick is just a kick."*

Part of the beginner's progression through these stages of learning and growth is that their frame of reference begins to expand and they become aware of how the new skills they are learning relate to experiences they have had in the past. In order to put these experiences into perspective, they begin to reference and compare what they are learning to past "wins" or past "losses." This identification with past experiences can work in a constructive way if their experience was a positive one. However, if their past has a negative connotation, it can have detrimental impact on their ability to learn.

In my own life, I have witnessed the difference in how I experience learning situations based on whether or not I allow past opinions and conditionings to cloud my perception of what I am doing. When I treat an experience as a totally new venture, free of comparisons and judgments of the past, I view it with excitement and openness and am primed for a great learning experience. However, when I correlate the introduction of new skill with the negative past, I can experience nervousness, frustration and even boredom. I am given the gift of seeing each new life lesson as an opportunity for growth and expansion.

In essence, this is about coming to new learning experiences with a "*beginner's mind*," letting go of the past so the entirety of the new experience or learning can stand on its own and directly integrate into our consciousness. My experience is that this holds true not only in martial arts but in almost any new experience and opportunity of growth and expansion.

Stage 2: Conscious Incompetence. *You know what to do, but you realize you cannot do it well, as you have yet to reach a level of proficiency.*

In martial arts, this is a critical stage. Students are beginning to see what needs to be done with their bodies on a mental level, but their bodies are not yet at the point of ability to execute due to limitations in strength, flexibility or coordination. As a result, frustration can reach its highest point. Many students ask the questions, "Is this something I can ever be good at? Why can't I get this down? Why is everyone better than I am?"

With those questions swirling in their minds, this stage is gut-check time in the student's quest for the Black Belt. It is easy to convince yourself that you cannot achieve something or you are not talented enough once doubt enters your mind. It is not that the lack of proficiency in body movement holds the student back at this stage; those limitations are slowly being lifted through practice, even if the results aren't apparent yet. Rather, it is the judgment and self-doubt residing in consciousness that can overpower the student and prevent him or her from transformation and expansion.

My good friend, speaker and author Craig Zablocki often asks his audiences these questions: "By a show of hands, who in the audience can paint a picture? Who can sing a song?" (I encourage you to ask yourself now, Are you able to paint a picture or sing a song?)

Usually only about 10 to 20 percent of the audience raise their hands. I suspect the majority, upon hearing the questions, immediately begin judging themselves as the voices in their minds say things like, "I am not an artist. I have a terrible singing voice. There is no way I would ever even sing in the shower, much less in public."

Now, imagine if you asked a group of kindergartners these same questions. How many hands would go up? Most likely all of them. Why is that? What has happened that we are so different from a group of five-year-olds? Did we somehow lose talent as we got older? Did we lose intelligence or ability?

Now imagine I had a thousand dollars in my hand and said, "Whoever can paint a picture or sing a song, I will give a thousand dollars. How many takers do I have?" I believe most hands would go up. When you examine these scenarios, it shows that it's not that members of the audience couldn't paint a picture or sing a song, it is that they chose *not* to.

All of us form beliefs and opinions of ourselves throughout our lives. Often, these beliefs are formed when we are very young when someone close to us, maybe a parent, sibling or friend, says something that told us, "You're not good enough. You're too small, too fat, too old, too young, not smart enough, not talented enough"—and we believed whatever it was.

For those of you who have children, you know how impressionable a child can be and how care needs to be taken in what you say to him or her. For example, tell children they are smart, talented and creative and they will most likely show up that way throughout their lives. Conversely, tell children they are slow, untalented and uncreative and they will demonstrate that in their lives.

What would you say if I told you I was putting a six-year-old in control of your life now? The child would decide what you did for a living, who you were in relationship with and what you ate in your diet. You would probably say, "No way—that is ridiculous!" Yet that is what we do when we hold onto beliefs formed at a young age and continue to bring them forward from our past into the creation of our futures.

Expansion increases with taking a deep introspective

look into these beliefs, so I ask you, "What beliefs do you hold that might be limiting you? What do you believe about yourself in your relationships, your career, your health and wellness and in your connection with Spirit? How are your beliefs impacting the way you interact with those around you, your spouse, significant other, your children, your co-workers or anyone you lead?" This is your opportunity to make a conscious choice as to what will serve you and what will not as you move forward. By being clear in choosing your beliefs you can transform your life and positively influence the lives of those around you.

Stage 3: Conscious Competence. *You know what to do, but you have to think about it.*

When students enter this stage, it is both taxing and ex-hilarating. When observing students move their bodies in a new way, it can be painful to watch as the frustration is evident. However, when they finally get it, even if they have to think about the process, a glow shines from them, radiating from their entire being. Here, too, students need to be in acceptance of the process and stay in alignment with their *Inner Champion.*

When I moved to Colorado several years ago, I took up skiing for the first time. As a competitive athlete my entire life, I had avoided skiing as an activity of impending danger of injury and I was constantly warned away from it by coaches. The mountains were now calling, and I felt it was time to take on a new challenge.

At first, I was excited. I loved the outdoors, and the thought of gliding down the mountain while the sun was shining seemed like heaven to me. What's more, my athlete's ego weighed in with the thought, "How hard could this be?"

During the first morning of ski lessons with a professional instructor, I learned how to snow plow, navigate the bunny hill with wide and gentle turns and bring myself to a complete stop. I couldn't wait to test my new skills on the easy, "green" runs.

The next step up in mountain grade brought a new set of challenges, however. No longer did I feel the safety and security of the instruction hill, and my frustration grew as my mind told me what I needed to do but my body did not seem to want to cooperate (I was in Stage 2). Here I was, a highly trained martial artist and former Division I college athlete, and I was stuttering and staggering my way down the hill as children flashed easily by me.

Feeling defeated and discouraged, I convinced myself I was ready for the clubhouse at the end of the next run. I also came to the conclusion that my young skiing career was about to end. As an adult, I had no need for this type of trauma and humiliation in my life.

Then I saw my five-year-old son, Jason, who also was having trouble navigating the hill in his first-time skiing experience. Like me, he was finding his joyous time in ski school crashing into an experience of pain, frustration and humiliation with each fall. As I witnessed my son crying harder and harder with each "failure" to remain upright on his skis, I realized that with each disappointment and frustration I demonstrated as I fell, I was giving him permission to do the same. I had allowed my own ego, which had told me that nothing but perfection would be acceptable as I went down the hill, to rob me of a potentially fun and enjoyable experience. What's more, by modeling this for my young son, I was showing him how to handle these challenges in the same way.

Then it hit me—what if I were to model the acceptance of imperfection for Jason? I had seen countless numbers of martial arts White Belts struggle with moving their bodies in new and different ways, and now was my time to show that learning a new process and making mistakes were not only natural and acceptable but could be fun as well.

I waited for Jason to "roll" downhill to meet me and suggested we move down the rest of the run together. This time, however, each time I fell, I let out a roar of laughter and smiled at him. Time and again, I made it up to my skis, went a few feet then fell in a heap, making each fall goofier and more playful than the last. At first, Jason looked confused (he probably was concerned his father had lost his mind), but soon he began to relax and mimic the behavior. With each fall to the snow, he smiled and laughed out loud. Soon it became a game to see who could demonstrate the most creative way of falling.

Eventually, the shift occurred. The falling became less and less frequent, and we were both able to go farther without losing our balance and taking our usual face plants. We quickly made it to the bottom of the hill and decided to go for yet another run. We put the second stage of Conscious In-competence and all of its frustration behind us and reveled in the third stage of Conscious Competence as we purposefully navigated the mountain, controlling our bodies with keen concentration on how to do so. Jason soon was off skiing and having a ball moving down the hill (Stage 4) as I continued to carefully, yet joyfully, control my body as I made my way down the mountain.

It is my hope that this story supports you when you have the opportunity to let go of the need to be perfect and surrender to the process of expansion. I have been blessed to promote hundreds of students to the rank of 1st Degree Black Belt or advanced levels of Black Belt. As I said earlier, those who have made it to these prestigious ranks most of-ten are those who found their training to be difficult or chal-lenging in the early stages. For those who are not naturally coordinated or athletic, something magical happens as they persevere in their martial arts practice. One day, their bodies start to understand how to move and execute a technique they have been working on, and a flash of accomplishment and self-worth engulfs them. From this euphoric state, they grasp the benefits of embracing the process over end results and continue on with deeper trust in themselves and their *Inner Champion* path.

What is so outstanding about this process is that it does not stay confined to the martial arts classroom. This same confidence and seeking to grow and achieve reaches out into other aspects of their lives and becomes their natural ap-proach to life.

Stage 4: Unconscious Competence. *You know what to do and you do not have to think about it.*

In this final stage of expansive learning, the newly acquired skill, habit or way of being has been integrated into your consciousness and happens automatically. It is not something that needs to be thought about before or during execution but moves freely once the intention to do so has been made clear. In martial arts as well as other disciplines, this becomes the state of "no mind." This is where the action actually becomes a form of moving meditation, and the practitioner can get lost in the motion or process and experience the feeling that time has stood still even when several minutes or hours have passed.

It is in experiencing this ourselves as well as facilitating this in others that we allow the process of moving out of our heads and into our hearts to occur. The net result is the realization of the highest form of efficiency and productivity. This state of oneness with the task at hand brings the greatest sense of joy and accomplishment. It is the work of the *Inner Champion* and the most impactful way of leading others with enthusiasm and confidence in the present moment.

Understanding that the Four Stages of Expansion is a natural progression for us to learn new skills and concepts can serve as a foundation for us to dramatically increase our ability to not only grow and expand but to fully integrate new learning into every aspect of our lives. By approaching new experiences with an open mind and heart, free of judgments based on the past, we make ourselves available to learning and experiences we may have never thought possible. In accepting that with growth comes the potential for both inner and outer obstacles to surface, it increases our ability to deal with them effectively when they do occur. Finally, in understanding that the road to mastery of any new skill requires us to consciously and patiently build our physical and mental capacities, we free ourselves to expand and grow.

5

COMPASSIONATE SERVICE

We must be silent before we can listen. We must listen before we can learn. We must learn before we can prepare. We must prepare before we can serve. We must <u>serve</u> before we can lead.

—William Arthur Ward

YOU MIGHT BE ASKING YOURSELF, "WHAT DO compassion and service have to do with martial arts?" Aren't the arts of Tae Kwon Do, Karate or Kung Fu disciplines that teach their practitioners not only how to defend themselves but also how to inflict bodily harm on their assailants if called to use their skills? This is certainly accurate, but the paradox of martial arts, as in much of life, is in mastering one element, we must understand its opposite. In martial arts, in getting in touch with the part that can administer physical damage on an opponent, the practitioner, if properly taught, gains a deeper respect for humanity and understanding of the sanctity of life.

This phenomenon is illustrated by examining history. The Hwa Rang Do warriors of the Korean Silla Dynasty in the Eighth through Tenth centuries were not only fierce gladiators but also were men of chivalry, strength and compassion who lived lives of service. Much like the legendary knights of King Arthur's Round Table, these warriors were skilled in the martial arts of hand-to-hand combat, sword play, archery and military horsemanship. They balanced these skills with education in painting, poetry and the healing arts.

Gichin Funakoshi, the founder of modern-day Shotokan Karate, was a master of the Japanese art of "empty hand" (Karate) fighting. He also was a high-ranking educator in the early 1900s who followed his vision for using the discipline of the martial arts as a means of character development in guiding the youth of Japan.

Morihei Ueshiba, the founder of Aikido, was once a teacher of a combative style of martial arts, but after a spiritual awakening, he changed his system to create an art, which is based on the principles of non-violence and service. His philosophical evolution in martial arts and life is stated in the following quote: "The Way of the Warrior has been misunderstood. It is not a means to kill and destroy others. Those who seek to compete and better one another are making a terrible mistake. To smash, injure, or destroy is the worst thing a human being can do. The real Way of a Warrior is to prevent such slaughter—it is the Art of Peace, the power of love."

All of these great masters saw the value of using their martial arts prowess as a means of evolving life and spreading peace. Their message of expansion and service throughout the world stands as the foundation of each martial artist's journey of self-improvement and actualization. The real lesson is that in improving yourself through study of the martial arts, you become much better equipped to make a profound impact on your world.

Fighting skills, physical fitness and mental toughness are by-products of the martial arts training experience; however, the most important result from this training is the growth and expansion of the *Inner Champion*. From the *Inner Champion*'s position of strength and compassion, students become ready to serve their fellow human beings on a much deeper and profound level. I consider teaching this message to be my most important contribution in my career as a professional martial arts instructor.

Although the physical accomplishments students achieve on their way to a Black Belt that I detailed earlier are outstanding, they are not what I am most proud of. Black Belt candidates are also required to complete a comprehensive curriculum in their personal development. They must do and record 400 random acts of kindness in the four-month training period. For junior students still living at home, 100 of those must be home chores (parents love me). They must mentor another person, either in school, business or martial arts, for ten sessions. They must read four inspirational books that focus on leadership and overcoming obstacles; they must right at least three wrongs and mend their broken relationships; they must meditate daily. They also must eat a clean diet for an entire week, staying clear of processed foods, sugar, caffeine and alcohol.

My favorite of the personal transformation requirements is what we call the "Day of Empathy." During their Day of Empathy, students must choose to spend the day being blind or deaf and mute or being confined in a wheelchair. The purpose of this exercise is for the student to experience first-hand the challenges of those with physical handicaps. For many students, this is the most powerful experience of the Black Belt candidacy process in awakening their sense of compassion and desire for service.

SEEKING FIRST TO UNDERSTAND: JOSH'S STORY

Josh came to my school when he was approximately 4½ years old and enrolled in our preschool martial arts program, Lil' Ninjas. A small, thin child with a bright mind, Josh struggled with coordination and control of his body. His floppy mop of red hair, freckles and glasses, and his habit of impulsively expressing his thoughts during class served only to irritate his martial arts classmates. Josh's uniqueness also caused him to be the target of bullies in his neighborhood and at school.

Josh persevered through the program and, after approximately five years of training, was accepted into the Black Belt candidacy program. He set his sights on testing for his junior Black Belt. Although his road had not been an easy one for Josh, as he overcame many challenges, he was determined to make his dream of attaining his Black Belt a reality.

As all students do, Josh experienced his own issues of personal challenge arising as he moved through the requirements of the program. Sometimes it was the mile run; other times it was fulfilling his requirement of daily push-ups and crunches; sometimes it was just getting himself to class when homework loads were heavy. However, in considering his Day of Empathy, Josh knew instantly what he wanted to do. Inspired by his Uncle Jimmy, a Vietnam veteran who was paralyzed from the waist down and had been confined to a wheelchair for as long as Josh had known him, he chose that experience. Excited to honor his uncle in this way, Josh shared his intention of spending his day in the chair.

Josh was surprised by his uncle's response. Uncle Jimmy told him that, although he was happy Josh had chosen this experience, he had an additional requirement for his nephew. His requirement was that Josh spend not just one day in the chair but two. Knowing Josh the way he did, he believed his nephew would find the first day in the chair one of play and adventure rather than truly understanding what it meant to bear a physical handicap. As a result, he would take Josh on a special field trip on his second day in the chair.

Josh's Day of Empathy came, and like so many students, he quickly began to realize the physical demands of his situation. Actions one takes for granted such as jumping out of bed in the morning, coming down the stairs to the kitchen to eat breakfast and hopping into the car to be driven to school all took four times as long and required a great deal of effort and concentration. He also found that maneuvering around school was difficult. Making it to class on time while negotiating the hallways during passing periods between classes, making his way through the cafeteria during lunch and, of course, using the bathroom, all brought their own set of challenges.

Josh went to bed that first night having gained a new understanding for what those with disabilities undergo every day. Little did he know how his appreciation and empathy for those confined to a wheelchair would soon deepen. On the second day, Uncle Jimmy arrived at Josh's house in his customized van, equipped with its mechanized wheelchair lift, custom-fitted accelerator and brakes and special seating for his chair. Within moments, Josh found himself being lifted into the van while seated in his chair via the electronic lift. A sense of nervousness filled him as he wondered about the day ahead.

Josh, his father and uncle soon arrived at their destination of Denver's Craig Hospital. Craig is regarded throughout the

Rocky Mountain region as a premier center for the training and rehabilitation of people confined to a wheelchair. At the rehabilitation ward, Josh saw men and women maneuvering in their chairs in ways he would never have imagined just to do the simple things so many of us take for granted. Josh was particularly mesmerized by one man who was a quadriplegic. Having no use of his arms or legs, he was learning to breathe from a tube in order to move his chair.

Back home, Josh excitedly shared with his mom and brother all he had seen. He went up to his room to write his required essay on his learnings. In it, he described how impactful the experience had been for him: He gained a greater understanding of the challenges others face while dealing with physical afflictions as well as a new appreciation for the full use of his limbs and senses.

Typically, Josh would have simply completed his essay and turned it in with the rest of his required materials as part of his Black Belt candidacy. However, he first gave his essay to his uncle to review. Uncle Jimmy was touched and inspired by what his young nephew had written and felt others would be as well. As an active member of the Disabled American Veterans, he submitted Josh's paper to the DAV's national headquarters. The folks there were so impressed with the essay they published it in their national newsletter.

Once the newsletter was distributed, word began to spread about the kid from Colorado and his powerful story. Someone realized that the DAV national convention was to be held in Denver that year and asked Josh if he would be willing to share his essay with their group. Josh proudly presented his paper to the delight of more than 250 disabled American vets. At the conclusion of his speech, he was met with loud and enthusiastic applause of appreciation. That year, Josh, not yet ten years old, had not only earned his junior Black Belt, but he was also a published author and keynote speaker.

I love this story. It brings joy to my heart that Josh was able to have such a deep and meaningful experience as part of his Black Belt testing. I also see his experience as an opportunity for powerful empathy awakening inside each and every one of us. He put himself in a position to open up his heart and mind to the deep lessons life had to teach. When we take the time to look at life from another person's perspective, we give ourselves the chance to do what author Stephen Covey identifies as one of his effective habits: "Seek first to understand, then to be understood." This important tenant, which we teach to all our martial arts students provides an internal guide for dealing with others in a loving and empowering way and sets the stage for us to make an important impact on our world through Compassionate Service.

THE NEED FOR COMPASSIONATE SERVICE

My job for ten years with the top consumer products company in the United States allowed me to represent good products and acquire valuable business education and training. The wonderful quality of people I worked for and with was second to none. When I left in 1995, it was bittersweet. I was excited to go out and live my dream, but I was sad to leave an organization and its people for whom I had such great respect and admiration. There was one instance, however, that made me realize it was time for me to move on from the corporate environment and pursue my own desires.

In my sixth year with the company, I was promoted to a special assignment for the company's world headquarters. I was charged with being the sales liaison on multifunctional teams responsible for bringing new products to market. These teams, which included representatives from branding, research and development, distribution and manufacturing gave me an intimate look into the inner workings of a major corporation.

My fellow sales special assignment counterparts and I were constantly under the evaluation of upper management, including our vice president of sales and brand group category managers. If I made the grade, I would be considered for positions of much greater responsibility in the company such as manager of a district sales office or key account manager for a major client.

One day, I was in a meeting room around a table with my vice president of sales and six of my special assignment counterparts. During an impassioned speech about the status of our business, our VP asked a simple question, "What is the purpose of our company?" Seeing this as an opportunity to audition and move up the ladder for the next available senior sales assignment, we responded with the answers we felt would best show consistency with the company line as well as impress the VP with our extensive knowledge and business acumen.

"The purpose of the company is to bring the best possible products to market," said one person. Another said, "To develop products with breakthrough technology to meet consumer needs." "To transform mankind by ensuring everyone on the planet has clean hair and white teeth." (OK, I made that last one up, but you get the point.)

After we had all provided our best answers, our VP sat up in his chair and leaned forward. While scanning our group with steely eyes, he said, "No, the purpose of this company is to produce profit for our shareholders."

I believe I am accurate in saying I was not the only one around that table who was more than a little shocked by that statement. Sure, we knew that making a profit was important. We all would not have jobs had the company not created enough profit to pay its employees. However, was this the main purpose of this fine company? Was this the primary reason for its existence? Had I invested the last six years of my life and career simply to line the pockets of investors?

I remember leaving that meeting confused and disheartened. There had to be something more. And if there wasn't, I needed to find something for myself that had greater depth of purpose than simply producing profits for shareholders.

GIVING AND RECEIVING ARE THE SAME ENERGY

According to noted psychotherapist Dr. Jordan Paul, being of service is an integral part of the journey of fulfillment. We have all experienced times in our lives when we were the beneficiary of acts of service. This might have come in the form of a caring act or a monetary gift when we were in need. Maybe it was a conscientious sales clerk in a store who helped us find the exact item we were shopping for. Maybe it was a teacher who helped us understand a concept we were struggling to comprehend. Or maybe it was a kind person who noticed our frustration and assisted us in figuring out the train schedule in a new city.

While being on the receiving end of service is a wonderful experience, I believe providing service to others can be one of the most rewarding and vitally important contributors to our growth and happiness. In his landmark book *The Seven Spiritual Laws of Success*, Dr. Deepak Chopra states the following about the importance of giving and receiving.

> *Every relationship is one of give and take. Giving engenders receiving and receiving engenders giving. What goes up must come down; what goes out must come back. In reality, receiving is the same thing as giving, because giving and receiving are different aspects of the flow of energy in the universe. And if you stop the flow of either, you interfere with nature's intelligence.*

According to Dr. Chopra, not only are giving and receiving one and the same energy, but they are also vital parts within the natural flow of the universe. The giving and receiving within nature is the basis for our planet's survival. For example, the rain falls on the earth to nourish the trees and vegetation of the forest. The sun shines to nourish the plants and causes the evaporation of the water back into the sky so that clouds may form and begin the cycle again. Each entity is in service to one another and each reaps the benefits of the other's giving and receiving.

Providing loving and impactful service to those in need can be one of the most important acts leading to the healing of our planet. However, it is my contention that in order to be of the highest service to others, we first need to take care of the only person in a position to offer service—ourselves. Loving self-care is absolutely essential if we are to truly give at our maximum level of loving effectiveness.

I want you to consider for a moment times in your life when you found yourself exhausted and depleted of energy. Maybe it was a time when you had immersed yourself in a project at work, spending several long days in a row at the office to meet a deadline. Or maybe you had just been blessed with your first child and found yourself serving your new bundle of joy day and night with feedings and diaper changing. How much energy did you have to give to others? How much patience did you have to truly listen to someone in need? How much strength did you have—mental, emotional or physical—to truly be with someone and serve them? Our ability to serve others is likely to be negatively impacted if we do not have the energy to make ourselves truly available.

So what are some of the ways you can support and nurture yourself? Could you do a better job of taking care of your physical self by eating healthier foods and exercising regularly? Are you getting proper rest each night? Are you taking time out of your day and week to rest and recharge so you can be reenergized and present when you are with others?

The secret is to find balance between nurturing ourselves and caring for others. In other words, we must learn to *take care of ourselves so we may help take care of others.*

MY SCHOOL OF COMPASSIONATE SERVICE

Service helps not only the receiver, but also the server. Whoever offers service must improve himself in order to do what has to be done, must think about others rather than only about himself. He learns. He finds value in what he does. Thus his self-esteem grows, and he is able to find meaning in his life. He enters into relation with another human being. And if, inevitably, he meets frustration, failure, or ingratitude, his motivation is put to the test and he has the possibility of emerging stronger for it.

—Piero Ferrucci, psychotherapist and author of
The Power of Kindness

In 1995, I left my position in that Fortune 100 company to pursue my dream of owning and operating a professional martial arts school. When I left, I took my years of business experience and success in a large corporate environment with me. I soon learned, however, that the world of small business was much different in one key area—guarantee of compensation. Although my salary in the corporate world was ultimately predicated on my production as a salesperson and performance as a manager and leader, if I ever did have an occasional setback and missed a sale or mishandled a customer issue, I still got paid every month. As a small business owner, my livelihood was dependent on the enrollment and retention of students. If I did not successfully make the sale of our program during the enrollment conference to the parent of a child, I did not get paid. In many ways, presenting to a high-level executive of one of my former corporate clients paled in comparison to sitting across the table from a mother of a potential student in my new career.

Soon after I opened my business, a woman called me to inquire about her 10-year-old son, Aaron, possibly participating in our martial arts program. As with any perspective student, I asked the simple question of his mother, "Tell me a little about your son. Is he shy or outgoing?" She explained how she, as a single mother, was looking for ways to support her shy son in gaining more confidence. She also made it clear that she was looking at several martial arts schools in the area and would not make a commitment to enrolling her son until she had checked out all the options. I told her I understood, gave her my point of view on what I felt was important to look for in a martial arts program and invited her son to attend our school for a trial lesson.

Aaron and his mom came to the school shortly after our conversation for him to partake in an introductory class. Aaron enjoyed his experience with us, but his mother still communicated she was looking at alternatives in martial arts education and that she would be in touch.

A couple of weeks passed and Aaron's mom returned to our center to enroll her son in our program. I was happy to accommodate the enrollment process. Before we started the process, however, Aaron's mom looked at me and asked, "Do you know why I am enrolling my son in your school?"

"No," I stated, "but I would love to hear."

She told me she had looked at several schools, some of which she liked and some she did not. What set us apart was what I said during our initial conversation, "Tell me a little about your son." She said we were the only center to ask about her son and his needs. All the other schools were interested in telling her about how great their programs and instructors were, but none seemed truly interested in her boy. That made all the difference for her.

This experience had a lasting impression on me. I clearly understood that showing care and concern for my students and sincerely inquiring about how I could meet their needs was paramount to the growth and success of my business. Showing concern and compassion for their well-being as people allowed me the opportunity to continue to serve them as my clients and, in turn, have the opportunity to make a lasting impact on their lives while fulfilling my desire of living my dream vocation.

OPPORTUNITIES TO SERVE

Now that we have Compassionate Service firmly in our consciousness, where can our energy be extended to help and serve others? Where are the opportunities to serve and how do we know where and when we can make ourselves available? These are questions I am often asked by my martial arts students.

Certainly, numerous opportunities to be part of teams that provide service exist at churches, charitable organizations, service organizations and schools. These are excellent places to make yourself available to make a positive impact. Numerous opportunities exist in our everyday life, too, if we become aware of them. In coaching Black Belt candidates in achieving their goal of performing 400 acts of kindness, I remind them of three steps to take.

1. Set the intention to serve. When we set the intention to serve and place our consciousness on wanting to provide help to others, we might be surprised what comes present. Simply saying to yourself, "I want to serve and am actively looking for chances to give back," creates an awareness that seems to magnetize these opportunities to us. It is similar to our example of getting clear about the make and model and/or color of car we desired then seeing them all over the place. Opportunities might come in the way of directly seeing someone who is in need, in the form of discovering an article in the newspaper or on the Internet, or through a conversation with a friend who suddenly makes you aware of a project. Remember, what you are looking for you will see.

2. Slow down. At times we are moving so fast, we completely miss opportunities to serve. How many times have you been walking into a store so intent on picking up what you had come to purchase that you were oblivious to what was going on around you? Slowing down gives you the time to simply observe. It also gives you the chance to connect with people and see where your assistance might be needed. Perhaps most important, slowing down allows you the opportunity to feel. When we are racing, we have a tendency to get into our heads and become self-absorbed. When we slow down and enter our heart space, the world begins to look different and we start to connect with others in a much deeper and more profound way and see where we might be of service.

3. Be courageous. Service from a heart-centered space can be one of the most rewarding activities we participate in. It might take courage for you to approach someone who looks as if they need assistance and ask them if they need help. It might take courage for you to take a stand for something you believe and join a group or organization that supports that cause. A natural tendency exists that brings up fear in approaching someone or making the commitment to a group to serve on an ongoing basis. My experience, however, is that when we make that leap, our rewards and satisfaction are always more than expected. Remember, courage does not mean the absence of fear; it means having the fear and doing it anyway.

Regardless of how you choose to serve, know that the actions you take have a ripple effect on our communities and our world. The phrase "think globally but act locally" says it well. The way we change our world for the better is taking loving actions right where we are now. I believe when the service-oriented actions of individuals reach a critical mass, they will serve as the tipping point in transforming our planet. As cultural anthropologist Margaret Mead so famously said, "Never doubt that a small group of thoughtful, committed citizens can change the world. Indeed, it is the only thing that ever has." Be part of the special group of individuals who is committed to making a positive change in the world. Allow your own *Inner Champion* to shine in Compassionate Service and watch your life and the lives of others transform.

6

ACCEPTANCE AND SURRENDER

Acceptance is the first law of Spirit. ... [L]ive your life in a state of Acceptance, which means Accepting yourself, others, the world, God and what is. There's no more argument with what is. We're talking about a state of awareness characterized by non-personality—about anything. The result is freedom from unwanted emotional suffering. And ironically, most areas of your life will improve, often including your physical well-being, your relationships and even your finances.

—Drs. Ron and Mary Hulnick

WHEN ONE THINKS OF A MARTIAL ARTS WARRIOR, the idea of surrender might not spring to mind. Warriors of any kind are believed to be strong and determined, with an indomitable spirit that carries them through the most challenging of life's struggles to victory. In martial arts, the physical demands of training have a distinct way of molding the practitioner into an individual who can overcome adversity and move through obstacles. In each class, students are pushed to their limits physically and mentally; in the process they are hardwiring inside themselves the ability to overcome obstacles in other areas of life. The idea of "never give up" is pounded into the students' psyches. In fact, I once had an instructor say to me, "Keep fighting until 5 minutes after you are dead."

The tenacity and never-die spirit of the warrior is known in Korean martial arts as the principle of *Pil Sung,* which loosely translated means "certain victory." But this does not necessarily mean meeting life's challenges with brute force. On the contrary, the most advanced warriors understand on a deep level the power of surrender and acceptance.

Surrender, as I am presenting it here, does not mean "giving in" to the obstacles or challenges that face us. It does not mean running and hiding from life's difficulties and shirking responsibilities for what we have created in our lives. I mean it as giving up or dissolving the patterns of behavior, struggles and beliefs that have caused these challenges to appear. In letting go we stand to gain a clear understanding of what we are working toward rather than fighting against ourselves.

In other words, it means giving up the fight in our minds so we may express in life through the power of our hearts.

One of my favorite movies is *The Last Samurai*. In it, Captain Nathan Algren finds himself a war prisoner of the last of the mighty Japanese Samurai leaders, Katsumoto. Held captive in an encampment for several months until the spring thaw makes the path back into the city passable, Algren is assimilated into the customs, traditions and martial arts training of this noble warrior clan. During one poignant scene, Algren is in a sparring match with one of the Samurai warriors, using his *bokken* (wooden practice sword) against his assailant's spear. Early in the match, Algren is being defeated easily by his adversary and clearly shows his frustration. After Algren is once again dropped to the ground, his new friend, house guardian and Katsumoto's son, Nobutada approaches him and speaks these words of wisdom:

Nobutada: "This for you; too many mind."

Algren: (puzzled) "Too many mind?"

Nobutada: "Hai. You use too many mind. Mind on the sword, mind on the people watch, mind on the enemy— too many mind." (seriously)

Nobutada: "No mind."

Algren: (pretending to get it) "No mind."

Algren goes back to the practice battle and brings himself to a point of center and "no mindedness." From this point, he fights valiantly until he finally is overcome by his opponent's superior skill. Regardless of the outcome of this match, the shift has occurred. Algren learns how to release himself from the entrapment of his thoughts and surrender to the power of his spirit. In doing so, he has found his *Inner Champion* and he is transformed in inner victory.

WHAT WE RESIST PERSISTS

Throughout the years, it has come into my awareness that we are a people who love to have a reason to fight. So many of the metaphors we use to describe our lives have to do with being engaged in battle. We battle our weight, our bad habits and our addictions. We fight traffic and in relationships and with our finances. On a larger scale, we engage in the war on poverty and the war on drugs. One who has been cured or is in remission of cancer has "beaten" the disease or "won the battle."

Please understand that I am not discounting the challenges these life situations bring; I have experienced or am experiencing many of them myself. Additionally, I have the utmost respect and admiration for those who have brought themselves back to physical, emotional and financial health and wholeness. I also deeply admire those who are committed to bringing an end to the suffering of others. However, I am convinced that seeing any of these situations as something akin to an enemy that needs to be defeated only gives the circumstance more power over us and substantiates and fuels its existence. In this way, the fight against unwanted circumstances is never-ending and actually perpetuates the very circumstances we are looking to eliminate.

For example, millions of dollars are raised and countless

hours of research and treatment are expended each year to defeat life-threatening or life-altering diseases. Battles are waged to keep drugs from crossing our borders, and programs are constantly being introduced and funded to conquer poverty. Although many who have been afflicted by these challenging circumstances have been helped, the conditions continue to exist and in some ways, thrive. Sadly, as author Dr. Wayne W. Dyer states, "What we resist, persists."

Decades ago, at the height of the Vietnam War, Mother Teresa of Calcutta is said to have been invited to a "march against the war." Protests against the war were at an all-time high with thousands, if not millions, of citizens across the planet demanding an end to the conflict and killing. When asked by supporters if she would bless them with her attendance, she flatly declined. Shocked by her refusal to participate in their worthwhile cause, the event coordinators asked her why she would not stand with them. Her reply was simple yet powerful, "If you have a march against the war, I will not participate, but if you have a march for peace, I will be there."

Mother Teresa seemed to truly understand the power of her actions and thoughts being focused on what she wanted to expand. She saw that surrendering this fight and focusing on the end result of what was truly wanted—peace in the world—would allow the war to diminish and "die," much like a plant that shrivels when it does not receive enough water. Unwanted or unpleasant conditions in our lives do the same if we surrender and accept them and stop resisting. Surrender and acceptance help us put our lives into a larger perspective.

IS THE TICKET GOOD OR BAD?

Sam was a middle-aged attorney living and practicing law in Southern California. He just completed the first of two meetings in Orange County for the day. The meeting ran later than expected, so he anxiously drove to his next meeting, which was being held near the LAX airport, some 35 miles away. It was early afternoon and the second meeting was scheduled to begin in an hour. He knew he would need absolute perfect traffic conditions to arrive there by the 2:30 p.m. start time.

As he turned onto I-405 going north, the flow of traffic was moving freely up the six lanes of highway like a sea of salmon moving upstream to their springtime spawning. With Hootie and the Blowfish blaring over his car speakers, he accelerates his Audi A5 Coupe to match the traffic's common speed of 75 miles per hour and clicked on the cruise control.

About 10 minutes into his journey, just as he settled comfortably into his mental rehearsal of his upcoming meeting's key points, he peered into his rearview mirror and saw the red lights of the California Highway Patrol flashing above the squad car directly behind him. Startled and exasperated at the same time, he pulled his car over to the shoulder, releasing a few choice words and a heavy sigh.

Sam watched the police officer approach his passenger-side door, with the sea of shiny, leased luxury cars zooming by him, accompanied every so often by pick-up trucks and semi-trailers hauling their loads.

"Good afternoon, sir. License, registration and proof of

insurance, please," the CHP officer requested.

Sam fumbled through the glove compartment of his car to retrieve the appropriate slip of paper and handed it to the police officer along with his driver's license.

"Officer," he said in a neutral tone, "with all due respect, I was going the same speed as everyone else on the road."

The officer nods and simply said, "Please remain in your car, sir." He then nonchalantly made his way back to his car to check out his information on the squad car's computer.

Sam grew more agitated by the moment, as each second that ticked away, his chances grew greater and greater that he would be tardy for his important client meeting. He felt the moistness of the perspiration in his armpits begin to grow as he continued to focus on the unfairness of his current situation and he remembered his client's story of how he fired his last lawyer for appearing uninterested in his case by arriving late to meetings unprepared.

The officer arrived back at Sam's car and presented him with a ticket for $200 for doing 75 in a 55-mph zone. Behind his mirrored sunglasses, the officer said, "You may pay the fine online by going to the CHP website. You seem like a very busy man, so it will definitely save you some time. Have a great day, sir."

With blood boiling, Sam made his way back into the flow of traffic. "At least traffic is still moving at a great pace. I should still be able to get there by 2:45," he said to himself as he reached for his cell phone to call his client to warn him of his impending tardiness.

Just as he found the client's number on his phone, all six lanes came to a standstill. Feeling defeated, he slammed his fists on the steering wheel, let out a scream and lay his head back on the head rest. Feeling the momentary calm that comes with resignation and without lifting his head, he reached to his car radio to find a traffic report. The traffic announcer related the news of a horrific 100-car pile-up ahead on the 405. Sam shook his head wondering what else could go wrong on this day and visualizing getting fired by his client.

In an instant, it hit him. Had he not been pulled over by the highway patrol and delayed for the 15 minutes it took to administer his ticket, he could have been right in the middle of the tragic crash. Upon realizing this, a wave of relief and gratitude washed over Sam. What once was considered an annoying experience had actually been a personal blessing.

As these stories so wonderfully illustrate, the focus of our energy and attention has a tremendous impact not only on what we create but how we experience it. We can't ignore the problems life presents us, but our setbacks and challenges often can be the greatest gifts life has to offer us. When we accept and surrender to what is, it opens up the space for us to create from a position of empowerment rather than struggle and resistance. This allows our energy to freely flow. From this point, the results are often better than we could have imagined.

ACCEPTANCE AND SURRENDER OF OURSELVES

Acceptance and surrender align with Being the Change we want to see and create in the world. Acceptance and surrendering to what is shifts our energy away from negative conditions and toward what we want to create. When we are able to accept this is the way things are, the energetic charge and internal struggle are dissolved in our consciousness, freeing energy we can use to focus on creating a plan of action versus staying stuck in the past fighting what we believe is the cause of our discomfort and displeasure.

Accepting what is takes courage and often means going against the conventional wisdom of the correct way to handle difficult or painful situations. However, the *Inner Champion* knows how to effectively channel his or her energy to move through obstacles. In surrendering to what is the warrior learns that the acts of acceptance and surrender are not signs of weakness but proactive means of empowerment.

Through this process, we learn that full and unconditional acceptance applies not only to situations and the behavior of others, but most important, to ourselves. Our "shadow" sides, the parts we like to pretend we don't have, must be accepted and embraced for the same reasons we give up resistance to conditions. These "bad" parts are aspects of who we are, and when we embrace these "dark" sides of ourselves and truly accept them along with our "good" qualities, we are set to live in fullness and wholeness.

The "warts on our skin" must be embraced and loved. For most of us, it becomes a conditioned pattern to project the source of our pain and suffering onto the behavior of other people or situations of the outside world. However, the true source of our suffering or discontent is always due to what is happening inside of us. When an internal voyage is undertaken, it is discovered that the turmoil that causes us suffering has nothing to do with the other person or circumstance. Rather, it is about how we are accepting the person we will always be in relationship with, regardless of the situation—ourselves. Full acceptance of ourselves is the first step in healing and personal expansion.

THE STORY OF THE WATERMELON BOY

When I was about nine years old, I had an experience that dramatically impacted me. As a result, I formed a self-image I would carry with me for most of my life. I was at my cousin's house playing with a group of six other kids. We were being led in our play by my cousin's neighbor, Johnny, who was a year or two older than I was. He was slender with brownish-red hair and freckles. He was also charismatic. Everybody loved Johnny and wanted to be like him. He was always the ringleader and would easily command respect with his wit and wisdom. Parents loved him, too, and he would often be seen doing his stand-up comedy routine for a circle of delighted parents during social gatherings.

I was quite different from Johnny. Even though I was a seemingly well-adjusted kid and a leader in my own right among my friends, it was easy for me to defer to an older kid. I did not have older siblings, so I enjoyed being the "little brother" and not always having to be the responsible one. Additionally, I often felt uneasy around other kids, as I was self-conscious about my weight. Although my mom called me "husky," it was apparent to me that other kids did not have the rolls of blubber on their stomachs and were not the butt of fat jokes. I was sensitive about being overweight and being called Chris "Fatzke," and it had a strong negative impact on my feelings of self-worth.

On this day, while the group gathered between play, we stood in a circle as Johnny once again held court. The subject of the day was "being in shape." Why this subject came up among a bunch of second- and third-graders I don't know, but it did. All of the kids stared in awe as Johnny described the attributes of the perfect male physique: powerful chest, large biceps, broad shoulders and flat, ripped abs.

I was particularly enraptured by his story. Having identified with superheroes, I had already made the correlation of the strong male body with the fight for truth, justice and the American way. Finally, my moment of truth came. Wanting so much to possess the characteristics he described and unable to contain my need to know, I loudly blurted, "Johnny, Johnny, am I in shape?"

All heads turned to me then quickly swiveled to Johnny, anxiously awaiting the words of wisdom from our childhood sage. He paused for a moment of reflection then a small smile came across his face. He delivered the words I can still hear almost forty years later, "Sure, Chris, you're in shape—like a watermelon!"

The words cut like a knife into my heart. Immediately, all heads in the circle turned back toward me, followed by the loud shrill of laughter and banter. I wanted to shrink up and die, but there was nowhere to hide. I was fully exposed as the fat boy I was, and now everyone knew it because it had to be true if Johnny said it was.

The subject matter changed and the group was off to the next discussion in a matter of minutes. However, the sting of those words stayed with me. I did *not* want to be Fat Boy or Watermelon Boy. I had to be the superhero and things had to change.

Soon, I began my martial arts training and, along with my growth in puberty, I slimmed down and transformed into a more athletic body. As my training continued and my body developed, however, I was still aware of the size of my waist and the tightness of my pants. This incident could be considered a positive happening in my life, as I became conscious of my level of fitness and took constructive action that led to my becoming a scholarship collegiate athlete and a national champion martial artist and instructor. As is often the case, our greatest strength emerges from what once was a great weakness. I now also believe everything that happens in our life is meant for our highest good, upliftment and growth.

However, for a long time, this was anything but positive. My self-image became imbalanced, negatively impacting my overall feeling of self-worth. The physical prowess I so dearly valued became my identity and my primary focus for how I saw myself in the world. If my physical condition was not at its peak, my self-esteem suffered. A few extra pounds, an extra increase in percentage of body fat or an extra inch around my waist became the catalyst for great concern and self-condemnation.

Furthermore, staying true to the regimented exercise and nutritional plan that maintained this physical state became so much of my daily focus that it negatively impacted my personal relationships with my family and my overall ability to enjoy life. Holding up the standard of the superhero I had hidden behind for so many years became exhausting. I was unaware my motivation had become nothing more than ensuring I never became the Watermelon Boy again.

I remember clearly when this finally came into my awareness and how it was negatively impacting my life. I was on vacation with my family at Disney World. As had come to be a common occurrence, I was stressing over the fact that I was again going to be missing a workout as we prepared to spend another day at the Magic Kingdom.   Suddenly, it hit me. By not being present to where I was, I was missing out on an amazing time with my family, specifically my two sons. In years ahead would I be unhappy with myself for missing a workout or would I regret the fact that I was not present with my children when we were creating these amazing memories together? I wasn't loved by my kids because I had less than 10% body fat. I was loved by my sons because of who I was on the inside and who I showed up being when I was with them.

Since then, I have come to realize that a self-image crafted in reaction to an external circumstance cannot be maintained indefinitely. Inside we will feel we are not good enough being ourselves but actually are only happy and satisfied if we are maintaining the image we feel we need to uphold. For this reason, accepting and truly loving ourselves just the way we are, is the greatest gift we can give ourselves. When we show up in the world from this place of acceptance within ourselves, we can truly access our Inner Champion. A sense of congruence becomes present inside of us. We can then Be the Change we want to see in the world and reach alignment with the Purposeful Vision we have for our lives.

STRENGTH COMES FROM VULNERABILITY

As a professional speaker, it is not uncommon for me to have several speaking engagements each week, sometimes even multiple speeches in one day. I have learned to welcome how often something that is said in an earlier session is perfect to be shared with another group later in the day.

One day, I had completed a talk for a local service organization on the importance of acceptance and surrender. While greeting audience members, I was approached by a delightful man who informed me he appreciated my talk and felt he was in alignment with the thoughts I had shared. He went on to inform me that for the past 25 years he had worked as a counselor in a drug and alcohol rehabilitation center. He said to me, "I agreed with everything you said; however, I think you need to remind your listeners that it is OK to ask for help. In all my years of treating others in my field, this is the most powerful lesson I have learned and can teach others."

I was moved not only by what he said but also that he had taken the time to share it. I made a commitment to him that in the talk I was giving later that day, I would be sure to share this point as part of my message. Committed to following through on my promise, I completed the second talk that day by sharing this experience and challenging the audience to learn when to ask for help, ensuring them that 100 percent strength comes from 100 percent vulnerability.

Not thinking much about the new ending of my talk other than the fact I was happy I had shared this new aspect of my message, I again greeted audience members. As I was interacting, I couldn't help but notice an elderly man making his way through the line to reach me. Looking to be in his seventies or eighties, he shuffled forward in short, halting steps, gently navigating his wheeled oxygen tank through the crowd with breathing tubes secured tightly in his nostrils.

The old man patiently waited for several people in front of him in line. Finally, he approached me with a calm yet inspired look in his eyes. He leaned toward me and said in a soft voice, "All my life, I had the best of everything. I had a wonderful career, a beautiful wife and kids, a great business and a magnificent home. I had everything. Then this happened to me," he said, pointing at the tubes in his nose. "I realized I had to ask for help."

His words touched me deeply. How many times in my own life had I struggled but refused to ask for assistance because of embarrassment, pride or my perception that others would find me weak, unqualified or inept. As leaders, we might resist asking others for their expertise, support or assistance because we feel we need to do it all ourselves to appear strong and worthy of leadership. However, my experience has taught me that when I ask for help, I am not only making myself more approachable and relatable to those I encounter, but I am also giving them an opportunity to express their strength, gifts and personal leadership abilities as well. We need to accept that we need help, accept that expressing our vulnerability is a strength and ask for what we need.

I challenge you—where can you ask for help in your life? Where would giving up the façade that you have it all together and under control and expressing your vulnerability serve you in showing you your strength? Find that area and try accepting yourself and asking for help. I am certain you will find it to be one of the most liberating and empowering experiences of your life.

FORGIVENESS

One of the most powerful examples of acceptance and surrender one can demonstrate is the act of forgiveness. The dictionary defines the act of forgiveness as "the act of pardoning somebody for a mistake or wrongdoing." In this definition, forgiveness is something we do to someone else. It is an act of releasing someone from a wrongdoing, hurtful action or mistake. In absolving someone else for their actions, we believe the situation of pain or conflict will be settled and we can move on with our lives. Seen this way, it is an external act, many times undertaken while maintaining a sense of righteousness as the one who is granting forgiveness to another who has wronged us.

When forgiveness is not granted, we create resentment and hold it inside of us. This resentment, when not released, builds up a tremendous amount of negative energy. Often this leads to a pattern of reviewing the perceived wrongdoings over and over, believing that reliving it in our minds will somehow allow it to pass or heal. We might also believe that holding the resentment toward another will somehow punish the perpetrator and allow us to get even. Although projecting our resentments in the form of angry behavior might negatively impact another, my experience is it usually has little impact on the target of our wrath. The person most directly impacted by one's resentments is oneself.

Consider for a moment that holding resentment has nothing to do with the other person. It might very well be that the resented person has absolutely no idea how you feel or no awareness of having wronged you in any way. An old adage states, "Resentment is a poison we drink hoping it will hurt someone else." But who ends up hurt? The person who swallowed the poison. What if forgiveness had nothing to do with the other person and everything to do with how we perceived the wrong inside of ourselves and what meaning about ourselves we assigned to it? What if the only person we ever needed to forgive truly was ourselves and the judgments against ourselves and others we hold onto?

There is but one simple truth, regardless of whether what happens is the tiniest of infractions or what is considered the most heinous acts: *There is what happens and there is the meaning we assign to it.* For example, consider you have a fight with a family member, say, your sister. In the heat of the moment, your sister recalls a moment from the past she knows will upset you and brings it forth as a means of neutralizing your argument. Upon hearing her words, emotions bubble up inside of you and you feel hurt and betrayed. The hurt is magnified as your sister used against you something you had shared with her in confidence. You had been extremely vulnerable in sharing it with her and now it is being used against you. You cannot believe how she could have said such a thing and you feel violated on a deep level.

As a result of the argument and your feelings of hurt, you decide to stop talking to your sister. A relationship that once was close is now basically nonexistent. Although you have given up direct communication with your sister, the argument lives on in your mind and life. Conversations with your spouse, mother and friends seem to always come back to the impasse with your sister, and you find yourself frequently reliving what occurred and sharing your pain and disgust with her behavior.

During quiet times alone, you review the events that occurred, searching for an answer that will relieve your pain, believing that proving yours is the correct position will somehow validate you. Resentment continues to build, dominating your thoughts and impacting your state of being until you begin to forget what it was like to not be angry and hurt.

Traditional forms of forgiveness would encourage you to simply let go of the matter and "forgive and forget." However, if the judgment placed against your sister is not resolved inside of you, there is a great chance that the upset will reoccur, if not with your sister, then with someone else playing the role of antagonist. The key is to take personal responsibility for your reaction and for the judgment you have placed against your sister. Once this is recognized and accepted, it may then be released.

The releasing or forgiving of these judgments is made within you. You are not really forgiving your sister at all—there's no need. You are, with great compassion for all human beings including yourself—forgiving yourself for the judgment you placed against her. This process of forgiveness is an internal practice called Compassionate Self-Forgiveness.*

In Compassionate Self-Forgiveness*, the focus is placed not on an act of perceived mistreatment but on the judgment you made of the person and more deeply yourself.

This is a startlingly new concept, so let's continue our example to see what it looks like in practice. In the traditional way of forgiving your sister for her actions, you might have expressed, verbally or in your thoughts, something that sounded like this:

I forgive my sister for being insensitive and divulging a secret to hurt me.

Do you see how this forgiveness is still directed outside of you and focused on the action of your sister? In Compassionate Self-Forgiveness, you would work with your judgments and arrive at something like these statements:

I forgive myself for judging my sister as insensitive.

---

*. Compassionate Self-Forgiveness is a process created and taught by the University of Santa Monica. To learn more about Compassionate Self-Forgiveness and its application and benefits, see www.universityofsantamonica.edu

I forgive myself for judging my sister as being untrust-worthy.

If you go even deeper, you'll see that the hurt is mainly from judgments you placed against yourself. These forgiveness statements may sound something like this.

I forgive myself for judging myself as unworthy of my sister's respect.

I forgive myself for judging myself as undeserving of my sister's consideration.

The very act of letting go of the judgments provides the opening for resentment to be released. Once the judgments of your sister's behavior and your self-worth are neutralized inside of you, upset dissolves. Once Compassionate Self-Forgiveness is done, true freedom and a sense of relief can be experienced. You are free to reconnect with your loving nature. This is the only true healing.

THE STORY OF THE TWO MONKS

Surrendering our attachments and judgments to what we believe is right and wrong and truly accepting what is can be the keys to allowing life to flow to us and experiencing deep peace inside ourselves. We can see this in the following story.

Two monks lived in a monastery on top of a mountain. Every five years, they were allowed to make a pilgrimage into the city below. One day, the two brothers set to make their way down the majestic mountain.

The monks' order was a loving and giving one. Their teachings were grounded in introspection and deepening their inner journey, and they also were involved in providing loving service to the mountain community where their monastery resided.

The order had one unique characteristic. Because their group was made up entirely of men, under no circumstances could any member have contact with a woman. They could not speak to women, they could not think about a woman, and they certainly could not touch a woman.

As the two monks made their way through a deep forest surrounding the city, they came to the river crossing. It was springtime and the winter snow had melted off the mountain so the river was high and the water moved rapidly. The monks looked at each other and wondered if they would be able to safely cross the river.

As they came to the river's edge, they saw a beautiful, young woman with long flowing brown hair and eyes that were as bright as the sun. She was frozen on the bank, too frightened to move across the dangerous river's flow.

One monk stopped for a moment, weighing his options, then he approached the young woman and warmly greeted her. He bent down, picked her up, placed her upon his shoulders and proceeded to carry her across the river. When they safely reached the shore on the other side, he gently set her down. She expressed her immense gratitude to him by giving him a warm kiss on his check and embracing him with a loving hug. They said their farewells and journeyed onward.

The other monk was following close behind and could not believe what he had just seen. His anger and frustration at his brother's violation of the order's sacred rules was intense. However, rather than voice his frustration, he decided to keep his anger inside, saying nothing as they continued toward the city.

The monks trekked for several miles as hours went by. The first monk was enraptured with the beauty of spring. The sky was a bright blue, a gentle breeze is at their back, and birds were singing. The second monk was agitated and angry with what he witnessed at the river, and his frustration built with each step he took. The fury inside him escalated until finally he burst out: "Brother, how dare you interact with that woman! Don't you know that speaking to her, touching her and allowing her to (gulp) kiss you violated every aspect of our sacred vows? How dare you act so disrespectful to our order!"

After a long pause, the first monk looked upon his brother with a warm smile and simply said, "My dear brother, I set the woman down hours ago at the river's edge and returned to observing all that is sacred here, but you appear to still be carrying her."

What are you carrying inside of you? Where does the opportunity exist to surrender the judgments that are holding you back and keeping you imprisoned? Are you drinking the poison of resentment hoping it will hurt someone else? I encourage you to explore Compassionate Self-Forgiveness. In doing so, you will truly release your *Inner Champion* and experience the fullness and wonder of life.

7

INSPIRED ACTION

Action is the great restorer of and builder of confidence.
Inaction is not only the result, but the cause of fear.
Perhaps the action you take will be successful;
perhaps different action or adjustments will have to follow.
But any action is better than no action at all.
—Dr. Norman Vincent Peale

LEADERS TAKE ACTION, WHETHER IT IS IN MAN-aging large organizations or their personal lives. The most effective leaders take Inspired Action, whether in massive efforts or incremental steps.

Grandmaster Jhoon Rhee stated that martial arts are an "action philosophy." I say the same holds true for leadership in life. Our world is full of individuals who have grandiose dreams but never have the courage or take the initiative to make them happen. Playwright and poet Václav Havel aptly communicated this idea when he stated, "It is not enough to stare up the steps; we must step up the stairs."

All of the previous Qualities of Black Belt Leadership come together to help us take Inspired Action and create what we want in our lives and make a positive impact in our world.

Let's look more closely at the dictionary definitions of these two words.

Inspire: "to influence, move, or guide by divine or supernatural inspiration"

Action: "the manner or method of performing."

To me, this is action propelled by the positive energy within us of our Purposeful Vision for full Self-expression.

Every day we take numerous actions. We get out of bed, brush our teeth, go to work, do our job, come home, eat our dinner and go to bed. For many, this cycle of activity can go on for years until we finally wake up and say, "Is this it? Is this all there is to my life?" The sober realization is that our song remains in us, unsung, never to bless the world through its expression if we don't change.

The reality of life is that Spirit—however you want to define or name the something greater beyond all creation—meets us at the point of action. Our dreams and aspirations have their origin in our minds and hearts. We must take Inspired Action to make them a reality.

MOVE THE BODY

Let's start with the body. Author and life coach Steve Chandler had this to say in his book *Time Warrior:*

> *Move the body and the mind and spirit will follow. Most of us have it the other way around. I know I did for years. I thought I always had to get it right in my mind and spirit before I could DO anything adventurous ... like go for a long run. Or create a successful career. ... But the body can go first. In fact, if I'll just do the thing, like Emerson says, "do the thing and you shall have the power," ...when I choose that route, it simplifies life and solves forever the "problems" of energy, purpose and enthusiasm.*

When I first read this quote, I must say I was somewhat conflicted. I had just completed writing about the importance of Being the Change and living a Be/Do/Have life. I was feeling good about what I had created and this seemed to contradict it. In the numerous keynote talks I have given, the Be/Do/Have philosophy is one of the cornerstones of leadership. It is also a concept I have repeatedly received feedback from audiences saying it was profound and transformational.

But now, Chandler was saying to move the body and the rest would follow. That seemed to be back to Do/Be/Have. Furthermore, I felt discontented as I realized in my own life how often I had decided to move my body first and let that momentum carry me to creating what I wanted in life. Almost always, getting going had resulted in experiencing the success and happiness I desired. What did all this mean?

After some deep contemplation, I understood an important distinction regarding this idea. I realized that when most of us use the word "be," we make it synonymous with the word "feel." For example, when first learning about the concept of *being*, students often understand this as how they are *feeling* about engaging in something. Therefore, they move forward with something only if they *feel* like doing it. In all honesty, waiting to do something until we feel like it is one of the greatest detriments to performance and creating what we want in the world and is closer to the Have component of our philosophy than the Be.

Deciding to take action in a new venture often has a way of bringing forward our feelings of fear. The fear of failure, the fear of being exposed and even the fear of success often come present as we move out of our comfort zones to experience expansion. When we feel these fears, it can be uncomfortable and paralyzing. Relying completely on feelings of discontent to pass before we take action is not the path to success.

As a dedicated student and athlete of the martial arts, I did not always feel like training. I did not always feel like stretching or kicking pads or doing forms (classical exercises) or sparring. However, what I found time and again, was the simple act of taking the first step in my training, despite how I was feeling, provided the momentum I needed to not only complete my training but enjoy it. Actually, when I felt the worst at the beginning but made the choice to move, I usually netted the most productive and enjoyable workout experiences. The motion served as the catalyst to create positive emotion.

I once heard a story of an elderly gentleman who had seemed to defy the laws of aging. In his early nineties, he still possessed a strong and lean frame with a strong chest and biceps and triceps a teenager would be jealous of. His legs and back were solid as tree trunks yet flexible and supple. A full, albeit thinning, head of white hair still donned his head, and he lived with a vibrancy of someone a fifth his age with a bright smile and twinkle in his steely blue eyes.

When asked what his secret was for his amazing physical vitality, he matter-of-factly stated, "I made a promise to myself over 70 years ago that each day I would do at least *one* push-up, *one* sit-up and *one* jumping jack." The questioner looked puzzled and the old man continued, "I knew that the first one was always the hardest, but if I could just get myself going, the rest would be easier."

Choosing not to take the first step due to fear or feeling uncomfortable is where many people make their biggest mistake. Do you remember George from a previous chapter? Let's return to him and his desire for better health. George looked at his routines, got a coach and had a plan to lose 30 pounds. He made a commitment to go to the gym and work out three days a week and began eating right to get to his ideal weight. At first, George was excited about his training plan and dedicated to his program, completing each gym workout and transforming his diet to one with lean meats, plenty of vegetables and fruits and healthy carbs.

After a week or two, however, he began to lose momentum and didn't *feel* as excited or dedicated to his program. Soon, he resorted to his old lifestyle and actually put on a few extra pounds. He felt guilty about not following through on his commitment to himself, and in his frustration the voice in his head began to say, "What's the use?" and he moved onto the next thing. Does any of this sound familiar?

Let's look at this scenario from the Be/Do/Have perspective. In this example, George wanted to *have* a greater level of health and fitness, and he decided to *do* an exercise and nutrition program that would support him in his quest for greater health and wellness. Sounds good so far, right? But here is the mistake that George and so many other people make. He confused his feelings with his way of being. He came to a point and said to himself, either consciously or unconsciously, "I don't *feel* like working out today" and decided to act upon his feelings rather than holding fast to the way of being he had committed to. In this example, he followed Feel/Do/Have rather than Be/Do/Have.

Steven Pressfield addresses this idea in his outstanding book *The War of Art*. In it he talks of the predicament many writers find themselves in when they say they only can write when they feel inspired. Pressfield quips, "I only write when I am inspired as well; it just so happens that I get inspired each day at 9 a.m."

Guess who holds the quality of Inspired Action for you? Your *Inner Champion.* When we are committed to Inspired Action, we succeed. Taking action for action's sake or moving only in areas we are comfortable in does not always net the results we desire.

BAZOOKA JOE WISDOM

When I was young, I loved bubble gum. My mom taught me how to blow bubbles with my chewing gum, and I loved showing off my skill in producing the largest bubbles possible without allowing them to pop and get caught in my face and hair.

My favorite bubble gum was the Bazooka Joe brand. Its flat, rectangular shape fit easily into my mouth, and within a matter of seconds, the sugary, pliable, pink substance popped joyfully out of my mouth. I also liked Bazooka Joe because of what was found inside each wrapper—a comic strip.

One day, I opened up a piece of gum and found a comic strip that had Bazooka Joe standing under a large streetlamp, feverishly looking for something. In the next frame, his friend Bill appeared and the following dialogue occurred.

Bill: "Hey, Joe. What are you doing?"

Bazooka Joe: "I'm looking for my keys."

Bill: "Want some help finding them?"

Bazooka Joe: "Sure, just go in front of my house to look because that's where I lost them."

Bill: "Joe, your house is five blocks away. If you lost them there, why are you looking here?"

Bazooka Joe: "Because it's totally dark in front of my house and I can't see a thing. But here, the light is amazing!"

How often to do we choose to take action on the things that are familiar to us because they feel safe and we can see what we have to do? I cannot begin to tell you how many times I got caught up in distractions and menial tasks during the writing of this book. I was taking action, but it was not inspired. I soon realized the familiar activities felt safe and allowed me to avoid my fears around being an adequate writer. When I remembered my commitment to my message, I was able to take Inspired Action and complete the book.

Take a moment and try a little exercise with me now. First, make a fist, gripping your fingers *over* your thumb. It does not take a Black Belt to know what would happen if you punched something with your hand clenched this way. You would break your thumb, correct? Let's take this a step further. What would happen if you practiced punching like this a thousand times? You would get really good at breaking your thumb. You can see how progress has nothing to do with taking action but is all about taking the correct, most productive action you know how to take at the moment. As we say in martial arts, "Practice does not make perfect; perfect practice makes perfect."

I now ask you, what are taking action on in your life? Where are you hiding behind comfortable behaviors or circumstances that are prohibiting you from really going for it and making your inner desires come into form in your life? What are the behaviors you are consistently practicing to make your dreams a reality? How could they be more inspired?

BLACK BELT CYCLE OF SUCCESS

Inspired by my dear friend Master Tom Callos, the Black Belt Cycle of Success has impacted the lives of thousands of martial arts students across the world with its direct, practical means of achieving success through Inspired Action. Study these steps to see how they can impact your life as they have so many on the martial arts path.

1. Know what you want. In using martial arts as a metaphor, we will use a student's road to the rank of Black Belt for this example. Because of the many years of training and skills that need to be learned and refined before someone can attain the rank of Black Belt, it is almost impossible that someone attains this prestigious rank without a strong commitment. The dedication necessary to achieve this rank requires students to make a definitive choice that they are set on achieving their 1st Degree Black Belt. They visualize what it would mean to them to have that belt around their waist, and they get very clear about knowing what they want.

In Chapter One of this book, we looked in detail at the elements needed to create a Purposeful Vision for your life.

As Dr. Roger Teel so aptly states, "Everything is twice created: first in the invisible mind and second as it comes into form." Let's review the three major components of a Purposeful Vision.

- *It comes from your heart.* A Purposeful Vision speaks to you and urges you to express from your heart. It continues to whisper to you as you encounter obstacles and contemplate quitting. There is a "coming from within" that drives any great vision.

- *It is clearly defined in your mind.* The greater clarity you have in your vision, the greater chance for success. This does not mean you should not be open to things coming into form beyond your vision as "this or something better." However, just as we would not begin a long trip without the use of a map, so our vision is used as a guiding force to getting where we want to go.

- *You become it on the inside before it happens on the outside.* Extraordinary visions might find their initial inspiration though the heart and mind, but they come to fruition when one embodies a "way of being" consistent with that vision. The story of Steven Spielberg "crashing" the Warner Brothers lot as a young man and taking residence in an empty office in order to "be" a movie producer is a wonderful example of someone who shifted his inner being then took action to make his vision a reality.

With the clarity of knowing what you want, miracles can begin to happen in your life. As author Stephen Covey says, "We may be very busy, we may be very efficient, but we will also be truly effective only when we begin with the end in mind."

2. Have a plan. No martial arts student, even with a vision, ever achieved Black Belt rank by just showing up and kicking and punching freely with no plan for progress. In the martial arts, most schools employ a belt ranking system to track the progress of its students. Each belt is anchored with its own curriculum of skills and techniques that a student must show proficiency in before moving to the next rank. The curriculum is the plan. It is the structure of education that guides the student from White to Black Belt to ensure all necessary skills are mastered to earn this prestigious rank.

Similarly, proper planning in life provides the structure for success in our endeavors. Action without a plan can often be wasted movement. Proper planning allows your energy to flow directly to the items most critical to your goal being realized. Any good plan for achievement breaks complex activities into steps that can be completed in progressive fashion. Henry Ford once said, "Nothing is particularly hard if you divide it into small jobs."

Before embarking on a major project, think of the end then work backward to break down the steps into manageable chunks that can be completed in succession and bring about your desired outcome. Remember to include steps for dealing with situations that might distract you from following the plan.

We discussed the quality of Integrity and the importance of honoring our word and keeping our agreements. When we do not do these, the cumulative effect of the energetic drain that occurs within us can be debilitating. As part of this process, you were introduced to the "5 D's of Keeping Agreements" (Detail It, Delete It, Defer It, Delegate It and Do It) as a means of gaining clarity on what items to commit to.

The "5 D's" process is highly recommended before embarking on any major project to loosen up and release any energetic drains or "incompletes" that might exist that would take your energy away from fully focusing on your project. It also helps you see what steps to include in your plan.

3. Have a success coach. Nobody gets to Black Belt alone. In addition to their primary instructors, each student on the martial arts journey has numerous people in their inner circle (parents, spouses, brothers, sisters and friends) who have supported them on their path. Some support them directly, some indirectly, but each plays a role in the student successfully completing the journey to Black Belt.

Talk to athletes of other sports and all would agree that direct coaching support is critical to their success. This certainly holds true for anyone undertaking a major project. Having a coach or an accountability partner that can hold you to your commitments to yourself and others is crucial to your success. As you are about to begin your project, seek those you trust and can rely on to help hold you to a standard that will produce the results you desire. Weekly or monthly check-ins can go a long way in ensuring you stay on track.

4. Take consistent action. Students reaching for the rank of Black Belt do not train in stops and starts. It takes a consistent effort of training several times each week over the course of at least three to four years to attain this rank. The same holds true for realizing success on a major project. Even when it appears something suddenly comes into form, it is usually the culmination of days, weeks, months or years of consistent effort that leads to the moment of accomplishment.

Progress toward and attainment of one's goals come from consistent effort broken down into the achievable chunks outlined in your plan. With each step, momentum builds and you are on your way. This is precisely why, when I coach clients who are looking to release weight and improve their physical conditioning, I recommend they commit to short, consistent, doable exercise routines (e.g. a 15-minute walk with calisthenics three days per week) rather than longer, more complex routines (e.g. six 90-minute sessions per week) when they start.

When you start slower and shorter, you will at least feel good about accomplishing your commitments. This creates positive energy inside you to apply toward your activity and possibly commit to more. Soon your routine becomes a habit you hardly have to think about but know you don't want to miss. On the other hand, if you overcommit at the beginning then fail to meet your commitments, you could get discouraged, lose momentum and possibly even quit.

I am reminded of a good friend of mine who often observed his father practicing daily calisthenics in their living room. One day, when he was a developing teenager, he teased his father about doing a relatively small number of push-ups. "Son," his father responded, "a little bit of something is better than a lot of nothing."

So get started small, be consistent in your action and remember, "How do you eat an elephant?" That's right—one bite at a time.

5. *Review your progress.* In the martial arts, students of the colored belt ranks generally have regular examinations to monitor their progress. Usually once per quarter, students are tested on their proficiencies; if they show competency in their skills, they are promoted to a new belt rank.

How often in life do we take time out of our busy worlds to review exactly where we are? Often our lives overtake us and soon we find months, if not years, going by without reflection on how we're doing in our lives and where we want to go.

With projects, take time each week to review your progress. Put on your calendar, each Friday, for example, to review the past week and check if you're on target with your goals. It doesn't take that much time, but the consistent effort of this task keeps your progress fresh in your consciousness and allows you to stay focused on your goals.

It's easy to find yourself off-course. In his landmark book *The 7 Habit of Highly Successful People*, Steven Covey used the example of a plane taking off from Los Angeles to Hawaii whose pilot allows the flight to be off by just one degree from its flight plan. Soon the passengers might find themselves landing in New Zealand rather than the Aloha State. It takes just a small degree of being off-course in life to find yourself in a different state than what you wanted. Have fun with the review process and see yourself reaching heights you only previously dreamed about.

6. Renew your goals. After receiving a new belt rank, the martial arts student sets their sights on their next goal up the belt ladder. A new Yellow Belt set his sights on the Orange Belt, the new Green Belt sets her sights on Blue. Taking the time to set new goals on an ongoing basis breathes life into your actions and keeps you focused on where you are going.

What we are discussing here is the power of setting intentions. In understanding that what we focus on expands and by renewing our goals, we are choosing where our energies will be directed and proactively creating the life we want in each moment. Dr. Roger Teel said, "An intention is an idea with clarity of purpose, and depth of conviction. We wrap an idea in that, and it is a power in the universe." Renewing goals through setting intentions keeps us moving forward in Inspired Action.

At the most fundamental level, with this approach, we are embodying what Viktor Frankl wrote in his book *Man's Search for Meaning,* "Man does not simply exist, but always decides what his existence will be, what he will become in the next moment."

TAKING INSPIRED ACTION

I have talked about the power of a Purposeful Vision and how that vision is best supported by truly empowering ways of being in connection with your *Inner Champion*. The final step is to take Inspiring Action, no matter how small the step. I encourage you to do this exercise to begin realizing one thing you want in your life.

Taking Inspired Action Exercise

1. Choose one thing from the eight areas of impact in your life you would like to achieve and write it below. Review the Chapter One discussion of the areas if you would like. The areas of impact are Relationships, Career Satisfaction, Service, Spiritual Connection, Health/Wellness, Material Things, Leisure and Financial well-being.

2. Next, from the work done in Chapter Two on Being the Change, write down at least three empowering ways of being you would need to embody to have what you want.

- _____
- _____
- _____

3. While keeping the big picture for what you want to achieve in mind, identify three Inspired Action steps you commit wholeheartedly to complete in the next month to move toward your dream.

- _____
- _____
- _____

4. Most important access your *Inner Champion* and continue Step Three each month until you have realized your goal. Continue to lean into your Purposeful Vision and allow it to become alive in your heart. Set daily intentions for the empowered ways of being you intend to embody. And whatever you do, keep moving forward each day in the direction of your dream. Remember: "Mile by mile, takes a while but inch by inch is a cinch."

DO IT ANYWAY

When it comes down to it, there are two basic emotions we follow or allow to guide our lives: love or fear. When action is not taken that we believe would best serve us, it is almost always a function of our being afraid to achieve our dreams. We might say it is due to timing or circumstances or not being clear, but the reality is there is some part of us that is holding back and not allowing ourselves to fully Self-express. However, when we are guided by love and allow ourselves to have the fear and do "it" anyway, magic happens in our lives.

To best illustrate this, I would like to offer you a poem often attributed to Mother Teresa. Her words stir me to take action when I find myself paralyzed by doubt, fear or concern. When I read these words, I become inspired to step through my greatest fears into action. It is my hope these words of clarity and inspiration have the same impact on you. Blessings on your path.

"Do It Anyway"
(Attributed to Mother Teresa)

People are often unreasonable, irrational, and self-centered.
Forgive them anyway.
If you are kind, people may accuse you of selfish,
ulterior motives.
Be kind anyway.
If you are successful, you will win some unfaithful friends
and some genuine enemies. Succeed anyway.
If you are honest and sincere people may deceive you.
Be honest and sincere anyway.
What you spend years creating,
others could destroy overnight.
Create anyway.
If you find serenity and happiness, some may be jealous.
Be happy anyway.
The good you do today will often be forgotten.
Do good anyway.
Give the best you have, and it will never be enough.
Give your best anyway.
In the final analysis, it is between you and God.
It was never between you and them anyway.

EPILOGUE

Becoming a leader is synonymous with becoming yourself.
It is precisely that simple, and it is also that difficult.
—Warren Bennis

ONE MORE PERSONAL STORY ILLUS-
trates the Qualities of Black Belt Leadership I have shared in
this book. Although I experienced the events as a young man,
their lesson has had a lasting impression on me and has been
instrumental in helping me live the principles of Black Belt
Leadership and inspire others to do the same.

It is the fall of 1980, a cool, brisk evening, and the crowd
is waiting in anticipation for a contest under the Friday night
lights. It is my senior year of high school football, and I am
captain of the varsity squad. Our team is undefeated at 6-0,
and I am preparing to lead my teammates into battle against
one of our conference rivals in our quest to the championship.

The mood in the team locker room is tense as each player
mentally prepares for the contest, some more than others.
I take this game seriously as the team leader as do many
of the other upper classmen. The younger members of the
squad, however, smile and snicker at each other nervously
and are the victims of my steely glares and those of other
team leaders.

Our head coach arrives and gives his final pep talk, reminding us of the importance of this game and what is at
stake. When he finishes, the room erupts in yells of confidence and commitment to the cause. Players begin scream-
ing encouragement to each other, banging their fists on each
other's shoulder pads and head-butting each other with their
helmets.

As team captain, I am to lead my fellow teammates out of
the locker room and down the 50-some steps onto the stadium

field. Starting cautiously at first not to lose balance, I begin to navigate the stairs and soon begin a light trot downward with my army of teenage gladiators behind me.

We stop at the edge of the running track that surrounds the field. Before us is the final obstacle we must maneuver before we enter the field in a blast of exuberance and confidence. The cheerleaders have constructed what they call a "run through." It is constructed of 2x4s, 8 feet high by 6 feet wide. A large sheet of butcher paper wraps around the frame with the message of encouragement painted boldly in our school colors of purple and gold: "Go Raccoons—Beat the Goslings!"

I let out a guttural battle cry and sprint toward the paper sign, my legion following closely behind. I powerfully blast through the sign to the roars of the home crowd. Nothing can stop me at this moment. I am invincible—or so I think.

What I neglect to remember in all my exuberance is the shallow drainage ditch of about a foot deep surrounding the entire field. Its purpose is to allow water to easily drain off the field when it rains or snows, and on some occasions, to make a fool of the overly enthusiastic captain of the football team. In an instant, the toes of my right foot catch the edge of the ditch and I trip awkwardly. Unable to regain my balance, I fall in midair amid the roar of the crowd and 45 rabid teenagers behind me.

As I fall, I feel held for a moment in suspended animation. It is as if time is standing still as I float in the air, my body horizontal to the ground. In that instant, two thoughts flash across my mind. First, if I fall now, I will create a scene much like a multicar pileup on the interstate, as my teammates awkwardly trip over me. Or, in the even worse second option, my teammates, in their frenzied state will not even notice me lying face down on the field and simply trample me to death. Not a great way to start the big game.

However, perhaps by some sort of divine intervention, I gain control of my thoughts, instinctively dip my shoulder, and without thinking, allow my years of martial arts training to take over. Before I hit the ground, I execute a perfect dive and roll forward, coming back quickly to my feet and resuming a full sprint with hardly a hitch in my step. Whew—disaster averted!

Once I regain my composure, I turn around to enthusiastically welcome my teammates onto the field, hoping no one has seen my near brush with embarrassment. What I see shocks and amuses me. One by one, each of my teammates is bounding onto the field with a forward roll, looking like a bunch of circus performers entering the ring.

To this day, the visual in my mind of that event brings a smile to my face. I learned great lessons that day.

Lead with purpose and enthusiasm.

Rely on your instincts and place confidence in your training and preparation.

As my college football coach, Dennis Green, once exhorted after a close win over an opponent, "Luck is when preparation meets opportunity." Believe this and others will follow—even if you are just making it up as you go.

As I reflect on this experience, I see how it became a living example for me of the Seven Qualities of Black Belt Leadership in action and is a template for how we all can choose to move forward in our lives.

The *Purposeful Vision* set forth by our coach and embraced by my teammates and me, led to an environment of achievement and success for our team. In the preseason months and throughout our season, our team chose the empowered way of *Being the Change* in embodying the commitment, enthusiasm, and courage that led to our success. As with any great endeavor, hardships presented themselves—in physical and mental fatigue, injury, challenging opponents and, yes, even in the form of an unseen drainage ditch—yet we each chose *Conscious Persistence* through these challenges. As a team leader, I learned that the best practice of *Compassionate Service* to my teammates was to think of their needs, give my all and lead by example. When fear and challenges arose, I learned *Acceptance and Surrender* to what was and relied on my instincts. Finally, whenever I was confronted with an obstacle, I called on my *Inner Champion* and practiced moving out of my head, taking *Inspired Action* and leading from my heart.

ABOUT THE AUTHOR

FOR FOUR DECADES, CHRIS NATZKE HAS BEEN A dedicated student and teacher of the martial arts, reaching the rank of 7th Degree Black Belt, Master Instructor as well as winning the United States National Championships in 1999. Prior to this, Chris left a very successful career as a corporate sales executive to create his own martial arts organization, the Colorado Alliance of Martial Arts.

In addition, Chris is a certified yoga instructor and the creator of Warrior TKD Yoga which combines disciplines of martial arts and yoga. He also has a master's degree in Spiritual Psychology from the University of Santa Monica.

As a keynote speaker, personal success coach and author, he has impacted the lives of thousands through his *Qualities of Black Belt Leadership*. Chris's message of inspiration, empowerment and belief in one's self inspires clients, readers and audiences to take decisive action in creating the careers, businesses and lives of their dreams.

Chris lives in Aurora, Colorado, and can be reached at www.ChrisNatzke.com

BLACK BELT LEADERSHIP
SPEAKING AND COACHING

WHEN MOST PEOPLE THINK OF MARTIAL ARTS, visions of fighting, competition and action movies may come to mind. However, at the core of martial arts training is a deep sense of commitment to personal excellence and giving back to the community and world.

Seventh Degree Black Belt, Master Instructor Chris Natzke uses martial arts as a metaphor for life. In sharing his "Seven Qualities of Black Belt Leadership" with individual coaching clients, businesses, organizations and their leaders, Chris demonstrates how these principles can positively impact the lives of others and set one free to experience the success and happiness they deserve.

To book Chris for your next event, contact him at 720-427-2835 or at www.ChrisNatzke.com

Made in the
USA
Lexington, KY